MW01289565

Morphic Fields Made Simple:

Find Love, Money & More

Michael Ambazac
Robert Mason

MORPHIC FIELDS MADE SIMPLE: FIND LOVE, MONEY & MORE

Published by Shelfless Ltd.

Copyright ©2013 Michael Ambazac, Robert Mason

All rights reserved.

ISBN 978-1491249482

First Edition (1) published 2013

www.MichaelAmbazac.com

This book may not be reproduced, in whole or in part, in any form or by any means electronic or mechanical, including photocopying, recording, scanning, or by any information storage and retrieval system known or hereafter invented, without prior written permission from the publisher, Shelfless Ltd.

LIMIT OF LIABILITY / DISCLAIMER OF WARRANTY: THE PUBLISHER AND THE AUTHORS MAKE NO REPRESENTATIONS OR WARRANTIES WITH RESPECT TO THE ACCURACY OR COMPLETENESS OF THE CONTENTS OF THIS WORK AND SPECIFICALLY DISCLAIM ALL WARRANTIES, INCLUDING WITHOUT LIMITATION WARRANTIES OF FITNESS FOR A PARTICULAR PURPOSE. NO WARRANTY MAY BE CREATED OR EXTENDED BY SALES OR PROMOTIONAL MATERIALS. THE ADVICE AND STRATEGIES CONTAINED HEREIN MAY NOT BE SUITABLE FOR EVERY SITUATION. THIS WORK IS SOLD WITH THE UNDERSTANDING THAT THE PUBLISHER IS NOT ENGAGED IN RENDERING SCIENTIFIC, LEGAL, EDUCATIONAL, OR OTHER PROFESSIONAL SERVICES. IF PROFESSIONAL ASSISTANCE IS REQUIRED, THE SERVICES OF A COMPETENT PROFESSIONAL PERSON SHOULD BE SOUGHT. NEITHER THE PUBLISHER NOR THE AUTHORS SHALL BE LIABLE FOR DAMAGES ARISING HERE FROM. THE FACT THAT AN ORGANISATION OR WEBSITE IS REFERRED TO IN THIS WORK AS A CITATION OR POTENTIAL SOURCE OF FURTHER INFORMATION DOES NOT MEAN THAT THE AUTHORS OR PUBLISHER ENDORSE THE INFORMATION THAT THE ORGANISATION OR WEBSITE MAY PROVIDE OR RECOMMENDATIONS IT MAY MAKE. FURTHERMORE, READERS SHOULD BE AWARE THAT INTERNET WEBSITES LISTED IN THIS WORK MAY HAVE CHANGED OR DISAPPEARED BETWEEN WHEN THIS WORK WAS WRITTEN AND WHEN IT IS READ.

Contents

PART ONE - FOUNDATION

INTRODUCTION

James Mattison is a 32 year old man living in England. He recently went through a difficult period. It started while driving home one evening, when an uninsured car drove straight into him. His insurance company refused to pay out for repairs, instead they wrote off his car. The same week, he was laid off from work. Living as he did in a remote village, he needed a car to be able to find a job. But without employment, he had no means to pay for one. His finances were already on a knife edge. Any money he had went straight towards paying the mortgage, otherwise he was in serious danger of losing his house as well.

Many people in James' situation might panic, or feel hard done by. But James wasn't worried, he knew he would be alright. One evening, at home alone, he closed his eyes, smiling to himself. An onlooker might have thought he was praying, or perhaps on drugs. But they would have been wrong.

Two weeks later, James received an offer of a new job. It was nearer to home than the one he had recently lost, and paid more. It also came with the benefit of a brand new company car. The extra money allowed him to make additional payments on his mortgage, giving him a safety buffer should anything untoward happen again in the future.

Alison Kemp is a 46 year old lady from Philadelphia. At about the same time James was being made redundant from his job, Alison's husband was telling her he was leaving her. They had been together for twenty one years, and she had always thought their relationship was rock solid.

But he said he was no longer in love with her, and was moving to California to start a new life.

Alison did panic. She loved her husband as much as the day she married him, probably even more so. How could she carry on without him? He was her whole world. After he packed his bags and left, she fell into a deep depression. She stopped getting out of bed in the morning. That lead to her losing her job. She failed to pay her rent months in a row, so her landlord started eviction proceedings. Life was becoming very bleak.

Fortunately for Alison, her closest friend knew what was going on. She had read something about a technique that she thought might help. She made some enquiries, and then went to see her friend. She convinced her to try the technique. With nothing left to lose, Alison decided to give it a go. With her friend in the next room, she settled down on her bed, gathered together a couple of objects, and closed her eyes.

Ten minutes later she emerged from her bedroom for the first time in days. Her face bore a wide grin, and she announced that she knew things were soon going to be okay.

Six weeks on, her husband Mark called her in tears. He told her he had made a terrible mistake, and begged her to take him back. She wasn't surprised, she had been waiting for the call. A month later they were back under the same roof, and their relationship was stronger than ever before.

Like James, Alison also quickly found new work, a job she enjoyed much more than the old one. With her salary and Mark's income, they were able to pay off the rental debts and remain in the apartment they loved so much.

What was the secret that James and Alison both knew? What happened when they closed their eyes, to make such dramatic and positive changes to their lives? Was it some kind of magic? To anyone who hasn't heard of morphic fields, it might seem like it. But the technique they were both using is firmly grounded in science.

Morphic fields are a new and exciting branch of scientific research. As with so much cutting edge science, there's much we don't know, plenty of speculation, and also a lot of misinformation. On the other hand, there is a lot about morphic fields that we understand very well indeed. Experimentation and practical application have enhanced our knowledge, particularly in the last ten years or so. With that knowledge, we are able to put these amazing natural phenomena to work for us.

In this book we're going to show you how to do exactly that. We'll start by explaining a bit of the science behind morphic fields. Don't worry, we won't go too deeply into it, our intention isn't to bore you to death with a lecture on quantum mechanics. But a basic grounding in what they are and how they work will help when it comes to use them.

Then we will get into the finer detail of how to make morphic fields work for you. You'll discover the methods you can use to control them, and some tips and tricks that will help you get up to speed quickly.

With the basics covered, in Part Two we will dive in and go in depth into a practical application for morphic fields—finding love. We sometimes call this part a 'love spell', because to the uninitiated it appears to work just like magic. Using morphic fields, you can make almost anyone fall deeply and genuinely in love with you. Even if you have no need of a love spell, the process we go through to make it work will give you an excellent understanding of how you can use the same techniques for other purposes.

One such purpose is to gain money, and in Part Three we will show you how you can adapt the same techniques used in the 'love spell' to attract money instead of romance.

Finally in Part Four we will look at other potential uses for the methods and processes you will, by then, be comfortable using. The sky is the limit when it comes to using morphic fields. Love, money, health, friendship, any positive outcome you desire can be obtained using the process you're going to learn here.

Resources

Occasionally we will make reference to further reading, useful websites, or other resources you may want to investigate. Rather than include links to these resources within the text, we will refer you to our resources webpage that accompanies this book. Experience shows us that websites change address or move pages frequently, rendering any links published in a book obsolete. Our resources page is kept up to date with any such changes, and we also add new and useful links to it as we come across them.

The address for the resources page for this book is:

http://www.michaelambazac.com/morphicfieldresources

About The Authors

Robert Mason stumbled into morphic field research quite unexpectedly. When a long term relationship ended, he became determined to win back the woman of his dreams. He tried all sorts of methods. Some were conventional, others, less so. A colleague knew of his troubles and introduced him to a man who claimed he could fix broken relationships with a kind of guided meditation. He had no idea how this worked, maybe it was the law of attraction, maybe it was a kind of self hypnosis. Morphic fields were mentioned. It didn't really matter, the fact was it *did* work. Robert met with the man on several occasions, and to his amazement, his sessions paid off. The woman he loved made contact with him. Before long they were back together, and their relationship was stronger than ever.

Most people would probably have left it at that, elated to have got their life back on track. But Robert isn't most people. He wanted to know what made the process function, the science behind it. For Robert is a scientist at heart, a believer in the scientific method of acquiring knowledge through experimentation, and the gathering of empirical evidence. His research has spanned many years. After quickly dismissing anything that couldn't be tested repeatedly, he focussed his efforts on studying morphic fields. As you will later learn, experimentation of this kind is not always easy. There are no instruments that can measure morphic fields at this time. So Robert used people. Of course, they were willing test subjects, he didn't just pluck them off the street! They were, like he had been, people who had somehow ended up alone, and who wanted to recover a relationship.

His initial results were promising, and through trial and error, he perfected a procedure that now has a simply stunning success rate. He has gone on to offer this procedure commercially. It's branded as a 'love spell', because to the masses, that's what it is. The results are akin to magic.

Literally thousands of people have used Robert's morphic field process with incredible success. It has brought joy and happiness where previously there was desolation and solitude.

Robert continues to research the field. He has used the same process he developed for relationships, to help people acquire more money, assist with heath problems, be happier at work, and countless other causes. Now he's sharing his knowledge in this first of its kind book, in order that more people can improve their lives with an understanding of morphic fields.

Michael Ambazac is a writer who is known for his work in more esoteric fields. He has published books on the tarot and on feng shui, among others. His fascination with these arts first began with numerology, when he was trying to figure out why, after a friend changed his name, a lot of other things about her life changed too. He studied numerology with one of the world's most eminent experts, and then went on to learn as much as he could about other metaphysical arts.

Like Robert, he wasn't content to leave it at that. Michael wanted to know what lay *behind* all of these diverse methods for divination and attraction. It seemed clear to him that there was some kind of uniting force that drove the effects, the arts all worked in such a similar way. When he discovered Rupert Sheldrake's research on the topic of morphic fields, he knew he had found his answer.

Also like Robert, Michael's research has been ongoing for many years. He continues to develop new ways of working with the fields. And now in this collaboration with Robert, you will find the tools to work with them too.

MORPHIC FIELDS

The term morphic field was first coined by British scientist Doctor Rupert Sheldrake. He has published a number of scientific papers on the subject. His work is fascinating, if somewhat dry and not always easy to read. The great thing about morphic fields though, is that you don't need to have a detailed understanding of them in order to use them. That said, the basics are easy to grasp.

A *field* is a kind of energy that can affect matter (or 'stuff' to use the less scientific term). We're all familiar with at least one kind of field—a magnetic field. Even though we can't see it, we know a magnetic field can affect certain stuff—metal. The dial on a compass moves because it is affected by the earth's magnetic field. And those little fridge magnets work because a magnetic field holds them tightly to the metal door of your refrigerator.

A morphic field also affects stuff. It's less fussy than a magnetic field though, because the stuff it affects is elementary particles. These are the smallest particles known to science. If you took anything in the universe, chopped it in half, and kept chopping the halves in half, you would eventually end up with a single molecule. If you kept going and chopped that up too, you would have some atoms. And if you chopped those up, you would be left with elementary (subatomic) particles like electrons and quarks.

These particles are what are affected by morphic fields. And because everything in the universe is built out of them, that means morphic fields affect *everything*.

They exist everywhere. They are inside you right now. And inside me. And inside this book. They are in the air around us. They are in space. They are in other stars and other planets. Morphic fields are themselves, part of the building blocks of the universe.

Properties of Morphic Fields

A magnetic field affects metal in that it attracts it or repels it, depending on the orientation of the field. What about morphic fields then? What effect to they have on matter?

According to Sheldrake, morphic fields are what organises matter into complex structures. The elementary particles that bunch together to form an atom don't just do so by accident. They are pulled together in just the right combination by morphic fields in a process called morphic resonance. The process infers that there is a form of communication between particles that is enabled by the morphic field. This communication is entirely independent of distance. A particle in your hand could be communicating with a particle in your nose, just as easily and instantaneously as it could be conversing with a particle in the sun, or a star in a distant galaxy.

It is this potential for particles to communicate with other particles that make morphic fields so useful to us. If we had a way to control morphic fields, we could control any particle. And as all matter is constructed from particles, that means we would have control over all matter, wherever it might be in the universe.

Clearly we don't have that kind of control (not fully anyway, as we'll see later). But we do have some influence over these fields.

Morphogenetic Fields

Some morphic fields can be influenced directly by living cells and organisms (which includes people like you and me). These are called morphogenetic fields. As their name suggests, they are found at the intersection of genetics and morphics.

Morphogenetic fields are thought to be responsible for all kinds of organising behaviour. It is believed that they have memory, that something that happens to one particle can be recalled by all others. This may explain why some people for example, believe that they have been reincarnated and can clearly—and otherwise inexplicably—correctly recall events from a past life. Events of which they could not possibly have any prior knowledge by 'conventional' means.

The implications of morphogenetic fields and memory are huge. It has been said that with a large enough database of information it would be possible to predict the future. If you knew everything that had happened in the past, and could access that information, collate it and study it, you could look for patterns. History shows us that events are often cyclical, they repeat in predictable ways. Wars often follow economic crises. Revolutions eventually follow unjust dictatorships. On a more granular scale, we can predict future weather based on information about how climatic conditions have acted in the past. As more and more information about the climate is gathered, and as computers become ever more powerful, so weather forecasts become more and more accurate (although it doesn't always seem that way!)

Now consider that all human experience is bound up and stored within the morphic field. Every action taken by every individual. Every thought anyone has ever had. Every decision ever made. With such a gigantic base of knowledge and shared experience available, it must be possible to predict the outcomes of any given situation or event with some degree of accuracy.

It is our belief that this is the means by which divination works. The memory of the morphic field has all the information, and the processing power, to come up with a likely answer to almost any question. Metaphysical arts like the tarot, numerology, or even reading tea leaves, are just a means by which we can access this information. As you will see, they are not the only means.

That's not the only property of morphogenetic fields though. The fact that these fields act on, and are influenced by, organic matter, and that we ourselves are made of organic matter, mean that we can—and do—manipulate them. Our actions and our thoughts touch the fields. They ripple out, into the universe. Everything you say, think or do, is connected to everything else, everywhere.

It's a pretty mind blowing concept, but physics has already proven to us that this is true. Quantum superposition, one of the fundamental principles of quantum mechanics, tells us that a particle such as an electron, exists in *all* theoretical states simultaneously. That means an electron exists here, there, and everywhere *at the same time*. It is spinning, and not spinning, at the same time. It sounds crazy, but it means that the very particles that make up you, me, and everything else, exist in you, me, and everything else, at the same time!

Only when particles are measured or observed do they fix themselves in one single configuration, which includes a single position. That's why we appear to have fixed physical forms, because we are ourselves, observers.

In practice what this means is that we can use morphogenetic fields to communicate with everything and everyone.

Morphogenetic fields are a subset of morphic fields. For the rest of this book will will use the term morphic fields, we don't need to get tied up in particular varieties.

You've Used Them

Did you know that you have already experienced communication through morphic fields? Actually it happens all the time. Most of the time we're blind to it. We send out and receive messages (thoughts) continuously, but because we aren't accustomed to using this method of communication, we rarely take notice. This is not surprising, as these messages bypass our conscious mind. Unless we've specifically told it otherwise, the subconscious, which is quite happily processing these communications, will just file them away somewhere they won't be seen. It's like an efficient personal assistant screening our calls. But every now and then one of those calls slips through. It's as if our assistant popped out to get a sandwich, or fell asleep at their desk. With nobody to screen the call, it gets rerouted to our main line of communication.

Enough theory, here's where you've experienced this yourself. Every once in a while, you'll find yourself thinking about someone. It could be someone you haven't seen in a long time, or maybe someone you were thinking you need to get in touch with. Your train of thought is interrupted by the telephone ringing. You answer, and lo and behold it is the very person you were thinking of. A shiver runs down your spine and you say "Oh, I was just thinking about you!"

This isn't coincidence, this is morphic field communication in action. The person who was about to call you, sent out their intention into the morphic field. They didn't do it deliberately, it just happened because, as we know, everything is connected. At the same time, your subconscious mind for whatever reason, decided to let at least part of the message through. Just enough that you started thinking about this person. And then the phone rang.

Of course these days this experience isn't limited to the phone. We've had test subjects and clients report the exact same phenomenon with emails, Skype calls, even posts on Facebook walls.

The 'intention to call' is just one example of how we pick up messages through morphic fields. There are plenty of others. Any time we find ourselves thinking of something, especially when we don't know why we are thinking of it, and then that thing comes to pass, it is our mind trying to relay what it has received. A very common example is having a song suddenly pop into your head, and then for that song to come onto the radio shortly afterwards.

Here's another example. Something that used to happen to Robert a lot would be that while out shopping, he would find himself thinking of something extra he and his wife needed, something not on the shopping list. Usually it would be quite an unusual item, not the sort of thing you would pick up every week. For example, a fresh coconut. I don't know about you, but we buy maybe one coconut a year on average, so it's not an everyday occurrence to be checking out different bottles of red wine in the supermarket, only to then have a sudden urge to go and pick up a coconut. To start with, Robert would dismiss these strange thoughts. But every time he did so, he would get home and his wife would say something like "I forgot to tell you, I needed you to buy a coconut." This happened so often (although not with coconuts every time!) that he started acting on these impulses, and purchasing the items he felt strange urges to buy. Imagine his wife's surprise when he began coming home with exactly the unusual item she realised she needed after he had left the house. Now that Robert's wife uses the methods you're going to learn in this book, she can 'send' him shopping requests at will.

We've yet to meet anyone who hasn't at some time in their life experienced this kind of scenario, be it knowing who's going to call before they do, intending to call someone only to have them call you first, or thinking of something that a partner or loved one is thinking about at the same time. Some people call this intuition. We have another name for it though, because we know what's actually happening to make it work. We call it *Passive Morphic Communication*. When you know about Passive Morphic Communication, or PMC, you can use it to your advantage, much as Robert did to delight his wife by fulfilling her unconscious shopping requests. But we can go further. Much further. When we use *Active Morphic Communication*, we take charge of the process. Instead of accidentally (or passively) stumbling over a subconscious message, we can deliberately (actively) send messages to intended recipients. Those messages can convey information and emotion. They can even promote behavioural changes, as you will discover.

CONTROLLING MORPHIC FIELDS

How exactly do we move from passive to active morphic communication? What do we need to do to take control of the morphic fields, to have them work for us? To find the answer we need to understand how PMC works.

Passive morphic communication doesn't happen all the time. As we've seen, it just seems to pop up every now and then. A lot of the time we aren't even aware of it until much later. Infrequent as it may be, it is possible to isolate the conditions present when PMC occurs. This formed a considerable part of our early research. There were a thousand and one variables to study to try and understand what common thread united instances of PMC.

The simple answer is that the people on either side of the communication—we'll call them the sender and the receiver—were in a relaxed state of mind. The complexity behind the simple answer is that there are many states the mind can be in. It's not as easy as relaxed and not relaxed, there are a lot of different levels of relaxation, a highly granular scale. It's a bit like different channels on a walkie talkie. There might be forty channels to choose from, and if the sender and receiver aren't both tuned in to the same one at the same time, the message won't get through.

So the next part of our research involved calibrating the levels of relaxation, and finding out which were most effective. As you can imagine, when dealing with a phenomenon that manifests infrequently, such research requires a lot of patience. What we found was startling to say the least. We discovered that at the right level of relaxation, the sender can get a message through to a receiver, without the receiver needing to be at the same level. This is like having a special channel on the walkie talkie that transmits to every channel on the receiving end at the same time!

Brainwave Frequencies

What is so special about being in a relaxed state of mind that it allows us to send messages? It's all to do with brainwave frequencies. Our brains work by sending electrical messages from one neurone (a special kind of brain cell) to another, along pathways called synapses. Our neurones are firing away all the time, sending messages around the brain, maintaining our bodies, thinking. We call the electrical signals caused by these neurones firing, *brainwaves*. They can be measured by electroencephalography (EEG). Like radio waves, brainwaves have a frequency, which is to say they occur a certain number of times per second.

The frequency of human brainwaves is not constant, it typically fluctuates between 1Hz and 20hz (one cycle per second to twenty cycles per second). Our brainwave frequency changes as we get older. Children's brainwaves occur at a lower frequency than those of adults for example. It also changes during the day and night. The frequency is not the same when we are awake as when we are asleep.

Broadly speaking, there are five bands of brainwave frequency, four of which we spend most of our lives operating at. These bands are as follows:

Delta (1hz - 4hz): This is the lowest frequency our brains operate at under normal circumstances. We experience Delta at least once every twenty four hours, when we are asleep. Not all sleep happens at this frequency, only the deepest sleep where dreams occur (also known as Rapid Eye Movement sleep, or REM sleep). Babies' brains operate at Delta all the time. It is possible to enter the Delta state whilst awake. Sometimes this can occur when we are particularly focussed on a task, but it is also possible, with practised mediation, to enter Delta at will.

Theta (4hz - 8hz): This is the level associated with lighter sleep. The upper frequencies of Theta occur when we are very drowsy, that moment between waking and sleep, just as we are dozing off. Again, practised meditation can lower the brainwave frequency to Theta. Very young children's brains operate at the Theta level.

Alpha (8hz - 13hz): A relaxed state of mind brings about the Alpha level. We enter Alpha numerous times throughout the day. When we first wake up in the morning, we come out of Delta, pass through Theta, then spend some time at Alpha until we are fully alert and active. The reverse happens when we go to sleep; we drop into Alpha as we relax, then doze off into Theta, dropping into Delta for periods of deep sleep. We also drop to Alpha when we are daydreaming, and when we are concentrating on something that doesn't require much brain processing power. Mowing the lawn, ironing, and washing up are all repetitive tasks that often lower our brain frequency to Alpha. Children's brains up to the age of about twelve operate at the Alpha level. Most coma patients also exhibit brainwaves in the Alpha frequency band.

Beta (13hz - 30hz): This is where we spend most of the waking day. When we are active, working, thinking about something in a structured way, talking or otherwise engaging with others, then our brains are at usually in the Beta band.

Gamma (30hz - 100hz+): The brain can boost itself up to higher frequencies on demand. This can happen when searching memory for specific information, and when processing information from the senses, particularly when lots of sensory information comes in at once.

If you think of your brain as a car, then Delta would be equivalent to having the ignition on but not yet having started the engine. Theta would be the state of your engine idling, but the car not actually moving. Alpha is like the car pulling away in first gear, and Beta would be like driving down the road on cruise control. Gamma is the equivalent revving the engine to the max and overtaking someone.

Alpha

The frequency band that is really of interest is Alpha, or 8hz to 13hz. Alpha is almost like a magic state of mind. You might think that as our brainwaves slow down, we lose concentration and can think less clearly, or process less information. But actually the opposite is true, to a point. The Alpha state is where our brains seem to work most efficiently. Going back to the car analogy, a car might well be capable of driving at 150mph, but it will usually be most efficient in terms of fuel economy, wear and tear on the engine and parts, and offer the smoothest quietest ride at around 55mph.

Brains are the same. The higher frequencies are useful for processing bursts of information. If we hear a loud noise and at the same time see something surprising (a firework maybe), then this double sensory input will send our brainwaves rocketing into the Gamma range as the synapses fire off in all directions, processing the extra information. All that data coming in from our senses is like lots of traffic on the road. We put our foot down, pull into the overtaking lane and zoom ahead. Once we've got past the traffic we can pull in again and carry on motoring at our normal cruising speed.

That's one way to process information, but it's not the most efficient. We end up changing lanes a lot, accelerating and decelerating. A better way is to be able to drive along at a lower but more constant speed. This is what happens when our brains operate in the Alpha band. They don't use up energy accelerating and decelerating. Instead, all of their energy and focus goes into processing the task at hand.

A lot of the time it doesn't feel like this processing is doing anything useful, after all, Alpha is where are brains are at when daydreaming, and that's not productive. Or is it? In fact, daydreaming is a highly creative state of mind. When we daydream, we create images, sounds, smells, and stories. We transport ourselves to other worlds. It's a process that sees all areas of the brain working together to create an alternate reality. And daydreaming isn't just about escaping from the real world, it's actually a way for our minds to find solutions to problems. Those problems can be trivial, like when we try and think of the word for something, or the name of someone, and it temporarily escapes us. We say: "oh it's on the tip of my tongue, it will come to me!" And invariably the answer comes to us when we're distracted, thinking about something else, or daydreaming. The problems can also be much more complex, such as making an important decision about a purchase, or a career choice, or a relationship decision. Any time we have a sudden lightbulb moment, when an answer seems to pop into our minds, or when we have a great idea that seems to come out of the blue, it's almost always while our brainwaves are in the Alpha band.

This is one reason why so many people find they are more creative in the morning, or have all their best ideas in the shower. These are times when we are naturally at the Alpha frequencies. Any time you're working on something (especially if it's something creative) and you find yourself "in the zone", in that state of mind where ideas seem to flow freely, everything just works effortlessly, then you are at the Alpha band.

Interestingly, going lower into Theta and Delta does not enhance the effect. With practice, it is possible to use these lower frequencies creatively, but it's very hard to do without going to sleep. Once asleep, obviously we have no control over what we want to think about, what problems we want to solve, or what ideas we want to come up with.

Alpha offers us a creative state of mind at a level we can consciously control.

So Alpha is a pretty amazing state of mind, but what has it got to do with morphic fields? All of our research and our testing with thousands of subjects has shown that we have the greatest power to influence morphic fields when our brainwaves are in the Alpha band. We've even narrowed it down to a particular frequency:10hz. It seems that morphic fields themselves resonate at this frequency (or a harmonic of it). By slowing brainwaves to the same frequency, those very brainwaves resonate and interact directly with the morphic fields. We can actually affect them just by thinking, provided our thoughts occur at the right frequency. We can initiate Active Morphic Communication at will. And the really amazing thing is that when we do so, the receiving person doesn't need to be tuned in to the Alpha frequency in order to pick up the message. The communication is so strong when we send it from Alpha, that it gets picked up regardless!

It gets even better. When we manipulate morphic fields consciously and willingly, we can achieve more than simple communication. We can set off all sorts of reactions. After all, morphic fields are present everywhere, touching every atom in the universe. We can interact with all of those atoms, and actually change their behaviour.

Of course, it's not quite as simple as just thinking about something and then it happens. There is a more structured approach than that, and we'll be looking at it in much more detail. But first we need to learn how we can lower our brainwaves to the Alpha band at will.

Reaching Alpha

The first step in using morphic fields is to lower brainwave frequency to the Alpha band. The closer we can get to 10hz the better. Without hooking up to an EEG machine we can never know for sure just what frequency we are at, but we don't need to be totally accurate, we can get close enough.

We've already seen how our brains are naturally at the Alpha frequency several times a day, the problem is that a lot of the time we don't realise we are in that band. When we're daydreaming, we are by definition not aware of the state we are in. As soon as we snap out of it, the Alpha state is lost. We cannot then, easily use daydreaming as a method for entering and utilising Alpha, because we need to be in full control of our thoughts if we wish to control and benefit from morphic fields.

The other times we are naturally in Alpha are just after waking up and just before falling asleep. These times can be used, with caution. During these periods we are often on the borderline between Alpha and Theta. If we don't have excellent self control, it is very easy indeed to drop too far into Theta and simply fall asleep. With practice, we can overcome that problem, and these in-between times can become productive. That still doesn't help us if we want to use morphic fields during the daytime. We need a way of getting to Alpha at will, and remaining conscious and in control once there.

Happily, such a way exists. It has been used for thousands of years by people from all over the world. It has been tried, tested, refined, and studied. It is not only useful for reaching Alpha, it also has great health benefits and is an all round good way to a healthier body and mind. I'm talking about *meditation.*

For some reason, mention meditation and a lot of people instantly tune out. Non-religious people think it is a religious practice, and so they shun it. Religious people think it is not compatible with their particular religion, so they shun it too!

It may be true that meditation has its roots in religious worship (there is evidence that prehistoric man used it when worshipping primitive gods), but the practice itself is entirely non-religious and non-spiritual.

We cannot emphasise this strongly enough. Meditation is purely and simply a mental exercise in the same way that walking is a physical exercise. Some people may choose to walk for days or weeks on end for religious reasons (a pilgrimage), but that doesn't make the physical process of walking automatically religious for anyone else. Walking is nothing more than the process of putting one foot in front of the other.

Meditation is nothing more than a mental process of consciously lowering brainwave frequency through relaxation. Whether you are a believer or non believer in any kind of deity, whatever your faith or lack thereof, meditation should not interfere with your beliefs. It is a benign activity that is compatible with however you choose to live your life.

Great, now we've got that out of the way, let's move on and see how we can use meditation to reach Alpha!

Meditation

There are many forms of meditation and they all have one end goal: to enter an altered state of mind by lowering brainwave frequency. Earlier we discussed how it was possible to enter Theta and even Delta band frequencies whilst awake. Meditation is the key to doing so. Entering such low frequencies takes skill and a lot of practice. Fortunately we don't need to go so low. Alpha is actually quite easy to reach.

Many of our clients, when first starting meditation, are concerned that they won't be able to do it. This stems from a misconception that meditation takes you to the same state of mind as hypnosis. In fact hypnosis requires delving down into the Delta band, it's a different kettle of fish altogether. If anything, the difficulty with meditating to get to Alpha is stopping at Alpha and not going too deep. This is where practice comes in. As with any skill, practice may not make perfect, but it certainly helps.

There are two ways we can meditate to reach Alpha: aided and unaided. Aided meditation is usually called brainwave entrainment. It involves the use of audio aids that train the brain to operate at the desired frequency. This is not the same thing as simple relaxation tapes or CDs, with sounds of waves crashing over rocks, or trickling mountain streams. Those can certainly help, but you are just as likely to end up in Theta, or asleep, by using them, as you are to reach the correct frequency level.

Instead, entrainment audio uses sounds with the same frequency that we need our brains to adapt to. Despite what we might like to think, our brains are easily manipulated. Play them a repeating sound at a certain frequency, and they will naturally 'tune in' and operate at that same frequency. This is perfectly natural and normal, there's nothing underhand happening, it's just the way human brains work. It's the reason listening to fast electronic disco music at 180 beats per minute gets the heart racing and the brain zooming along, whereas a classical piece at 50 beats per minute is relaxing, to the point that it will send some people to sleep. The brain just follows along with the frequency of the music.

In aided meditation, or brainwave entrainment, we can't use an audio sound with a frequency of 10hz (the ideal frequency for morphic field manipulation), because that's so low it is outside the range of human hearing. We can however, cheat. By using a multiple of that frequency (called a harmonic) that we *can* hear, we can trick the brain into going down to 10hz. It's a bit like taking a piece of music that was written for a bass guitar and playing it an octave or two higher on a lead guitar. The notes are the same and the piece sounds the same, just higher up.

To use an audio aid then, we must listen to a repeating sound at a harmonic frequency of 10hz. The sound should not be played so loud as to become a distraction, it needs to be background noise. Loud enough that it gets through to our subconscious. An ideal way to do this is to overlay another sound on top. This is where those crashing wave CDs can be useful. Hiding the harmonic frequency under the sound of the ocean means that the conscious part of the mind will listen to the sea while the subconscious will fix onto the harmonic sound.

If this all sounds complicated and like a lot of work, don't worry. On the resources page for the book we've provided a link where you can download just such an audio file (several in fact). Listening to one of these in a quiet room with no distractions, and with your eyes closed, will on its own, bring you pretty close to the Alpha level.

Unaided meditation is the ideal, and should be your goal if you want to make use of morphic fields regularly. If you become adept and practice daily, it is possible to close your eyes and reach the Alpha band in a few seconds, no matter where you are. Even on a packed commuter train, or a bus, or in a crowded bar. Wherever you find yourself, you will be able to shut out the world, without being dependent on audio aids.

We highly recommend starting out using aided meditation with a harmonic audio combined with the exercises we're going to teach you in the next section. It will be like learning to ride a bicycle with stabiliser wheels attached. It makes the process easy and you'll be able to get around immediately, but at the same time you'll be learning the right actions so that when the time comes, you can get rid of the audio 'stabilisers' and go it alone.

The Heavy Body

The first meditation exercise we use is called the heavy body. This isn't something you will be using for connecting to morphic fields, but it's an exercise to get you used to relaxing your mind. It's a bit like doing sit ups or bench presses if you're a long distance runner. If you're not used to running, you would need to do some basic fitness training before embarking on a marathon, otherwise you would just end up doing yourself an injury.

Meditation is similar (although happily there is no danger of hurting yourself!) Most people have no idea how to really properly relax their minds. We might think we are good at relaxation, but usually when we talk about chilling out or taking it easy, we mean sitting in front of the television, or playing video games, or going out with friends. These activities are as far from true relaxation as it is possible to get. They are simply a different form of stimulation from whatever it is we spend the rest of the day doing.

True relaxation involves quietening the mind, emptying it of thoughts, letting it float free. Michael clearly remembers the first time he tried meditation. It was the most freeing experience of his life. It was as if he had opened a door into a new world, a paradise that he could shape and mould into whatever he wanted. Our clients often tell us the same thing, that learning to meditate opens their eyes to just how much is going on in their heads the rest of the time. One person told us:

"It was like finding out I'd been living in a nightclub since the moment I was born. I hadn't known anything different. But the first time I tried your meditation exercise, it was as if the DJ turned off the music, everyone stopped talking, and the doors opened, letting in the light. For the first time in my

life I understood the noise that had been in my head since the day I was born. In fact, it was like being reborn into a new, silent, better world. It was such an incredible sensation I wanted more. I couldn't wait to do it again, and again! Now I meditate every day, several times a day. I honestly don't know how I ever managed before."

This is a common reaction. We've had people ask us if they are in danger of becoming addicted to meditation, such is their desire to do more of it once they have discovered the deep sense of inner calm and peace that it brings. But that's like asking if you can get addicted to breathing. Not only is it a healthy thing to do, we believe it is essential to leading a normal balanced life.

The heavy body exercise then, will introduce you to mind relaxation, perhaps for the first time. Before you try any of the other meditation methods in this book, you should do this exercise at least once. It's a good idea to keep doing it at least once a week, even when you use other, simpler methods more frequently. It is a way of keeping in shape. Here's how it works.

Firstly, you need to find a comfortable quiet spot, somewhere you won't be disturbed by external noise or other people. The exercise takes about half an hour, so if you live with other people, try and find a time when you know they will leave you alone long enough. Try not to get too comfortable though, or there is a good chance you will fall asleep during the exercise. Sitting in a nice chair is ideal, but if you prefer to be lying down on something that's okay too. Keep your arms and legs uncrossed. Ideally you don't want your arms or hands touching any other part of your body. When you are ready, you will close your eyes. Take a deep breath, then let it out slowly. Concentrate on the breath, try not to think about anything else. When you have done so, you should then focus on your feet (stay with us here! We know this might sound weird, but it works great.) You want to literally focus your mind entirely on your feet. Without moving or touching them, just try and feel them. It could well be the case that you feel nothing, or that you are just aware they are there and no more than that. There is no right or wrong way to do this, just follow the process. When your mind is fully occupied with your feet, tell yourself (in your head, not out loud) that they are starting to become heavy, very heavy. Concentrate on that feeling of weight. Tell yourself they are made of lead, they are so heavy, you can feel them sinking into the ground. Take your time, don't rush this. Your feet should actually start to feel heavy, but again, don't worry if they don't, it might not happen for you the first time (or even the first few times) you do this. Just keep going through the exercise, you will get better every time. After a couple of minutes focussing on your feet and telling yourself how heavy they feel, you then tell yourself that you can no longer feel them at all, that they have become detached from your body and have floated away. Again, whether or not you get this sensation doesn't matter, with practice it will come, and amazingly, it really will feel like your feet are no longer there. We know that for some people, the first time this happens they freak out a bit, it's so unexpected. If this happens to you, you can always open your eyes and check that they haven't really gone anywhere. This applies throughout the exercise. If you feel nervous, worried, or uncomfortable at any time, you can simply open your eyes and stop. You cannot, however, close them again and carry on where you left off. Instead, get up, walk around, take a break, then come back to it and start the exercise over.

After your feet have drifted away and are no longer (in your mind) connected to your legs, you can now repeat the process with your calves—your lower legs. You will go through exactly the same steps as before. Focus your mind on your calves, to the exclusion of all other thought. Then tell yourself they are becoming heavy, incredibly heavy, as if made of lead. Feel them weigh down, sinking into the ground (or the chair, etc.) And then when they have become really heavy (or after a minute or two if this doesn't happen), tell yourself you can no longer feel them at all, that they have become detached and have floated off.

You will keep repeating this process, working your way up your body. Your knees, thighs, bottom, pelvis, hips, belly, chest, hands, arms, shoulders, neck, face, ears, and finally your scalp, the very top of your head.

A number of things could happen as you progress through this exercise:

• Stray thoughts might enter your mind, breaking your concentration. This is not only very likely, it is almost inevitable, particularly if you are new to meditation. It is not a problem in the slightest. Instead of getting annoyed or distracted by a thought that comes along, simply acknowledge that it is there, and then release it. Just let it go, move on with the exercise. Even if you feel like you have taken a step backwards and become less relaxed, don't worry about it, let it go and carry on. Like we say, this is to be expected.

• You may fall asleep. This is very common if you've never done anything like this before. It's not a bad thing and it doesn't mean you did anything wrong, it just means your mind isn't used to relaxing properly. Next time you try you'll probably get further through the exercise.

• You might get all the way through with nothing happening at all. Again, this doesn't mean you did anything wrong. When nothing happens it's usually because your mind is so unused to relaxing that it actively rebels and refuses to do so. Continued practice of the exercise will eventually break down this mental blockage, and when that happens you might find you fall asleep during the exercise. That's a great sign, it means your brain is learning to let go.

• You could end up feeling like you have no body and that you are floating in space. You may even feel dizzy, or that you are flying around the room uncontrollably, or that you have somehow left this world and gone somewhere else. This can be accompanied with a feeling of euphoria or unbridled joy. If this happens if means you've become fully relaxed and are probably in a Theta state, possibly even Delta.

• The last possibility is simply that you feel exceptionally relaxed, but fully in control of your thoughts. In this case you are almost certainly in Alpha, probably towards the lower end of the frequency band.

Getting to this relaxed state is not the end of the exercise though, you need to bring yourself back out of the meditation. Whilst you could simply open your eyes, get up, and go about your business, this is really not recommended. Doing that can be quite a shock to the relaxed mind, and whilst it won't physically do any damage, it can leave you feeling groggy, confused, or light headed, as if you've taken painkillers or sleeping tablets.

To exit the meditation correctly, you must count yourself out. To do this, you first tell yourself (again, in your head not out loud), that you are going to count from one to ten. Say to yourself that when you reach ten you will open your eyes and feel wide awake, alert, and better than you have ever felt before. Then, start counting in your mind. Do this slowly. Say the number in your head, and if you can, try and picture it too. When you get to five, remind yourself that at ten you will open your eyes and be wide awake. And of course, when you get to ten, you should open your eyes. When you do so, say to yourself *out loud* that you are wide awake and alert and feeling better than ever.

To make this easier, here's a sample 'script' of what you would say to yourself in your head to count yourself out of a meditation. It's worth learning this and memorising it because you will use it in all the other meditation exercises and methods in this book.

Count Out Script

[To be said in your mind, not out loud]

"I am going to count from one to ten. On the count of ten I will open my eyes and will be wide awake, alert, and feeling better than I have ever felt before.

One…

[Pause for a couple of seconds between numbers, try and picture the numbers as you think them]

Two…

Three…

I'm coming slowly out of my meditation…

Four..

Five…

On the count of ten I will open my eyes and will be wide awake, alert, and feeling better than I have ever felt before.

Six…

Seven…

Eight…

[Take a deep breath and hold it]

Nine…

[Let out the breath at normal speed]

Ten.

[Say this out loud with conviction:]

I am wide awake, alert, and I feel better than ever before!"

Concentration Techniques

For quicker meditative exercises you can use any time you have a few minutes spare, you can use the concentration technique. There are several varieties you can use, and you can create your own as well. We will look at two common methods here. Both work very well, the second is more flexible as you can do it anywhere at any time.

Like the heavy body method, these exercises are about training your mind to reach the Alpha band with ease. The more often you use them, the easier your mind will find it to relax on command. And as with the previous exercise, we recommend you try these with a harmonic audio track playing if you can.

Candle Concentration

A classic technique for relaxing is candle concentration. The object is to empty the mind of all extraneous thoughts by filling it with one simple one. Quietening the mind in this way is a sure-fire way of reaching Alpha.

As you have probably guessed, you will need a candle. Literally any kind of candle will work. Short and fat, long and thin, scented or plain, whatever you have handy will work just fine. All we are interested in is the flame itself. The exercise works best in a room without draughts, as we want the flame of the candle to stay relatively stable, not be blown all over the place.

Find a comfortable sitting position. Light the candle and place it in front of you, somewhere you can see it easily. Not so close it burns your nose, and not so far you have to squint to see it. Obviously you should make safety a priority. Ensure the candle is held securely in place by something. You may well fall asleep during the exercise, you don't want to wake up to find your home burning down! If you can, place your arms and hands by your sides. Your legs should not be crossed. Take a deep breath and let it our slowly. This naturally starts to lower the brainwave frequency as you deprive the brain of oxygen. Now, focus on the very tip of the candle flame. And that is it! You want to try and block out all other sensory inputs. Ignore sounds. Ignore any other movement you might be able to see in your peripheral vision. Ignore any smells. Just focus solely and wholly on the very tip of the flame.

If, as is likely, any thoughts enter your mind, acknowledge that they are there and then let them go peacefully. Just bring your thought and focus back to the tip of the flame.

Try and focus on the flame for as long as you can, several minutes at a minimum, and up to five minutes if you can. The more you do this the better you will get and the longer you will be able to focus. You may want to set an egg timer or an alert on a cellphone to let you know when your time is up.

When you are done, it is best to count yourself out. Even though your eyes are open for this meditation, you will be in Alpha and counting out will help bring you back to Beta and will, as a bonus, give you an energy boost. Close your eyes and use the script you memorised for the heavy body exercise.

Once you've completed the exercise don't forget to blow out the candle - safety first!

Focussed Breathing

This exercise is very similar to candle concentration. Instead of focussing on a flame, we centre our attention entirely on our breathing. The advantage is obvious; there is no need to have a burning candle around and so the exercise can be practised anywhere at any time. It requires more concentration as there is no physical object to actively focus on. While that makes it a little more difficult, that slightly higher skill requirement means that if you get it right, you will achieve a very high level of focus and concentration.

The method is very simple. The exercise is best conducted with your eyes closed as this will block out visual stimuli. Begin by taking a deep breath and letting it out slowly. Then start breathing rhythmically. Do this by counting in your head as you breathe. Take an in breath through your nose, and count to four as you do so. Hold the breath in and count to four again. Then breathe out counting to four. Your out breath should be through your nose, but if you prefer you can breathe out through your mouth. Count to four once more, then start the cycle over.

Each count of four should take around four seconds. Don't get obsessed over precise timing, if you need to breath a bit faster then do so. The actual length of time each breath takes isn't as important as the fact that each part of the cycle takes about the same amount of time. But the most important part of all is that all of your attention is on your breathing. As with the previous exercise, you should attempt to ignore any other input or stimulus. That doesn't mean actively try blocking them out, that would require that you devote some mental energy to the task, which in turn means you wouldn't be focussing fully enough on your breathing. Instead, just let noises, distractions, and stray thoughts float over you. By all means notice them, but let them past without engaging them in any way, as you might let someone running up stairs pass if they are going much more quickly than you.

Visualisation

Before we move on to other meditation methods that we can use to quickly reach the Alpha band, we need to step aside and discuss the second technique that is essential if we are to be able to manipulate morphic fields. That technique is visualisation. Once we are Alpha, we will use visualisation extensively. But we can also use it to help us reach Alpha.

Put simply, visualisation is the process making a mental image of something. If we said to you "Think of an elephant", you will somehow in your mind, 'see' an elephant. However, and this is important, not everyone will 'see' in the same way.

Visualisation is badly named, because it suggests the process is inherently visual. That is not necessarily the case. Some people do visualise in a visual way. They will literally see the elephant in their mind's eye (note the expression 'mind's eye' is also misleading!) But someone who is more auditory will 'hear' the elephant. And someone who is kinaesthetic will just be aware of an elephant, perhaps its shape, or simply its presence or size. The point is that to visualise, you don't have to make actual images in your mind.

Even people who are visual by nature (for the vast majority of humans, after all, vision is our primary sense), sometimes have problems visualising. Or rather, they think that they have problems. That's because another popular misconception surrounding visualisation and the mind's eye is that when you imagine something you are supposed to 'see' a beautifully rendered High Definition three dimensional image. Or that when you visualise you should see pictures as if you were in the cinema. This is not how visualisation works for 99% of the population. The images you see or sense could be blurred, or vague, or just outlines, little more than ideas. This is fine and perfectly normal.

That said, not everyone uses their imagination very often, so there are exercises we can use to improve and enhance it. Again, like physical exercises, the more regularly these are done, the greater the effect will be. The exercises can be done at any time you want, they won't take time out of a busy schedule. The ideal time is when you are already at Alpha during a meditation, but you could just as easily do a quick visual warm up whilst taking a shower, or waiting in line, or sitting on a bus. A great time to try this is just before you go to sleep. You'll naturally be falling into the Alpha band anyway, so you'll have a head start (the imagination works much better at Alpha).

At the very least, we would recommend you do these exercises every time you do the heavy body meditation. Once you've reached the top of your head and are floating in space, stay there a while and work on your visualisation. Take as long as you need, and when done, you can count yourself out. Any other time you want to do an exercise, just close your eyes and go for it. The more frequently you try, the better you will get. And the better you get at visualising, the more success you will have at using morphic fields to get whatever you want from life.

Visualisation Exercise One

Close your eyes. Think of the house or apartment in which you live. Try and imagine that you are standing outside facing the main entrance or facade. With your eyes still closed, count the number of windows in the building. Take as long as you need to do this.

Of course you will be counting these from memory, and you might not 'see' the windows. That's fine, however your mind chooses to count the windows is how your brain chooses to visualise.

Now imagine that you have just entered your home. Take a mental tour of where you live. Walk around and count the number of doors you have to go through to visit every room. If you have a small or open plan home with no doors, you can do the same exercise using someone else's home, or a place of work, anywhere you are familiar with.

Once you've done this exercise a couple of times you will obviously know how many windows and doors there are without counting, but don't let that stop you repeating it. It's not about the answer, it's about getting to the answer through the active use of your imagination.

Visualisation Exercise Two

When you are happy that you can do exercise one successfully, you can drop it and move onto this second exercise.

Close your eyes and imagine you are standing outside the main entrance to your house or apartment. Picture the most prevalent colour of the exterior. For example, if the building is brick built, the main colour will probably be red or yellow). With that image firmly in your mind, count to three, and on the count of three, in your mind's eye, change the colour of the exterior to green. Hold that image in your mind for several seconds. Then count to three again and on three, change the colour to blue. Repeat this exercise several times, changing the colour to whatever you want (but always decide before you count to three what the next colour will be, don't make it random).

This can be a much more difficult exercise if you are not used to working your imagination. It isn't just about imagining colours, it is about control. When you have an image in your mind and you tell yourself that you are going to change the colour, your mind will naturally try and see that colour immediately. You have to try and hold it back, to only allow the colour to change on the count of three. Success in this exercise then, isn't measured by being able to see your home in different colours, but in your ability to change the colour on the count of three and not before. You will probably need to repeat the exercise a number of times over a period of several days before you become proficient. Although it can be tempting to move ahead to the next one before you're ready, do try and avoid that temptation. The next exercise moves up another notch in difficulty, so you'll be doing yourself a disservice if you cheat!

Visualisation Exercise Three

Close your eyes and picture a large figure 8. The figure should be entirely in isolation, nothing else around it, in front of it, or behind it. We specifically use 8 and not another figure because it has a very distinct form and is relatively easy to visualise. At this point you don't need to worry about the size or colour of the number, or the colour of the background it is projected against, just use whatever comes to mind first.

With the number clearly in mind, you can start to take control of it. Begin by changing its colour as you did with your house in the previous exercise. Again, decide the colour it will become first, count to three, and only then allow it to actually change colour. This may be a little tougher than with your house because this is a partially synthetic image. In the previous exercise you were able to recall an image of your house from memory. This time round, although you know what a figure 8 looks like, you have created this particular one yourself.

When you are done changing colours a few times, start to play with the figure in other ways. Move it towards you, then away from you, and 'observe' the effect that has on its size. Turn it upside down slowly. Rotate it. Try changing its texture. If it is smooth, give it a rough finish like sandpaper or concrete. Change the colour again and observe how the new texture reacts to the new colour. All of these changes should be done on the count of three and not before. Again, this isn't just about imagining colour and movement, it is just as much about exercising control over those attributes.

Visualisation Exercise Four

This final exercise will combine all the visualisation skills that you have practised thus far, and add a new one; creation. Although you created your figure 8, it was still based on your knowledge of what the number looks like. Now we want to create something truly unique, a real product of your imagination.

Close your eyes, and imagine that you are standing in your kitchen (or any other room if you prefer). Count to three, and on three, imagine a figure 8 in front of you. It should be the same height as you, and at arms length from you.

So far we have been concerned with the visual (even for non visual people). Now we're going to add other elements. Before starting the exercise, pick a song or piece of music that you like and know well. With the figure 8 in front of you, count to three and on three, the 8 itself will start playing this music. The sound will appear to emanate from the number. As the music plays, change the colour of the 8 in time to the rhythm.

You might need to do this exercise more than once before you are happy that you can imagine a musical figure 8 in your kitchen. When you can do so with relative ease, take the exercise even further. Reach out and touch the 8. How does it feel? Is it rough or smooth? Hard or soft? Does it move when you touch it? These are no right or wrong answers to these questions, it is your imagination that will decide.

Try picking the 8 up and moving it. Is it heavy? Or light and easy to move around? Perhaps it was already floating in the air, or maybe it seems to be fixed to the floor. If you can't move it, try walking around it instead. Observe the rear side. Is it different in texture? Colour?

Now that you've really got your imagination going, we can take things to the next level. You are going to imagine that you are shrinking in size, like Alice in Wonderland. Everything around you, including the 8, appears to be getting bigger and bigger as you get smaller. Keep shrinking yourself until you are about the size of a mouse. Then walk forwards until you are standing right in front of the (now giant) 8. Reach out and tap on it three times. On the third tap, a door will appear in it (but not before). Push the door open and step inside. What's it like in there? Dark or light? Does the music sound the same, or is it echoing around? Does the inside seem smaller than you expect, or bigger? Perhaps there is a party going on inside, and all your friends are already there waiting for you. Or perhaps there is nobody, just a lot of scaffolding and ladders holding the figure in shape. Is there a way to get to the top? If not, just fly up there, after all this is your imagination and you are not limited by such trivialities as gravity. What does it smell like inside? Fresh and clean? Or damp and musty? Use all of your senses to explore the space fully (try licking the walls, taste is an important sense that can really work the imagination!)

This Isn't Work

There really is no limit to how far you take that last exercise, or any other you choose to create. Try and make it fun and enjoyable. Exercise is one of those horrible words that makes the activity sound like hard work, and it doesn't have to be. The more you enjoy using your imagination, the easier you will find it.

You should work on one exercise at a time, and try and do it at least twice a day, every day. It will only take you maybe five minutes each time, and is well worth that tiny effort. When you are competent in one exercise, drop it and move on to the next. When you've done the last one to death and know everything there is to know about the inside of your figure 8, make up your own new exercises. By then your imagination should have been set free and you will be able to create all sorts of new and interesting scenarios to play with in your mind.

Performing the exercises will help tune in your imagination. You will find that each day you will get better and better, you'll have more control over what you're doing, and you'll be able to do it more quickly. Don't worry during the exercises if you find you cannot do any of them, or you cannot control the mental images, this is all just practice and as long as you stick with it, you will get better. In fact, you cannot fail to improve.

Countdown Meditation

Now that you have got some experience of relaxing the mind using the exercises we looked at earlier, and you have also sharpened your visualisation skills, you are ready to move on to the primary meditation. This is the meditation technique you will use every time you want to connect to the morphic fields in order to do something, whether that be attract someone, obtain something, or change something. Like all good meditation techniques it is simple and very effective. It combines everything we have learnt so far; relaxation, breathing, and visualisation. All three elements will help you reach the Alpha band quickly and easily, and the visualisation element will 'warm up' your mind's eye, ready for the visualisations you will be doing once at Alpha.

As with the previous methods, you should start by finding a comfortable position, somewhere where you won't be disturbed or distracted. Your legs will be uncrossed, and your arms by your sides, your hands not touching each other or any other part of your body if possible. If you have been practicing the other meditations, you should now have good control over your mind and be able to relax without going too far and ending up in Theta or sleep, but you may want to set an alarm just in case.

When you are ready, close your eyes. Take in a deep breath through your nose, hold it for four seconds, and then let it out slowly over four seconds. Now continue to breath normally but slower and shallower than you would otherwise. In your mind's eye, picture the figure 9. I'm not going to tell you what size to make it, or what colour, texture, or any other attribute, you should use whatever comes to mind and that you find easy to visualise. However, once you have decided, you should visualise the number in the same way every time you subsequently use this meditation. Each time you do so you will be training your subconscious mind. It will begin to create an association between your numbers and the Alpha band, and eventually just visualising these numbers will take it to the correct frequency effortlessly.

When you have the figure 9 in your mind, imagine a spotlight being switched on, its beam focussing on the top of the number. Now move the circle of light over the figure, tracing its outline. Again we are being deliberately vague about the type of light, the colour, and how it moves over the nine. These are all things you can decide for yourself, because then they will be something you can easily picture. And if you prefer to imagine the number being painted bright pink, then by all means do that. The aim here is to focus all of your attention on that number, and to make it memorable. This will relax the mind, slow the brainwave frequency, and create an association that will make the process more effective the next time you do it.

When you have finished tracing the number, make it disappear and think of a number 8. You will repeat the same steps as before, tracing the outline of the figure in your mind. You don't have to make your number eight the same style, or colour, or size as your number nine, and you don't have to use the same method to trace it if you don't want to. However, we would highly recommend you do make all of these numbers uniform in those respects, otherwise you will have a hard time remembering what each one looks like, and if you have to start searching your memory for information, your brainwave frequency will increase and you will leave the Alpha band completely.

When you are done with the eight, repeat with a figure 7. And then a 6, and so on, all the way to 1. Take as long as you need on each figure, but try and keep the pace constant. If you stop and spend too long on a number you will be in danger of letting your mind wander, which is the opposite of the objective.

By the time you have reached the number one, you will almost certainly be in the Alpha band. Closing your eyes and slowing your breathing are enough to get you most of the way there, the numbers are a belt and braces means of ensuring you arrive at just the right frequency and stay there. In parts Two and Three of this book we will examine in detail just what you will do once you reach the Alpha band using this method. For now, if you want to practice this meditation, once you get this far you can remain at Alpha and use it to practice complex visualisations such as visiting the inside of a number. Time spent at Alpha is never wasted, it is a very healthy state of mind, and can help your physical wellbeing too.

When you are finished practicing visualisations, or have completed your morphic field work, or are simply done relaxing, you can count yourself out using the same count up script we have already discussed.

Routine

As we have already tried to stress, continued practise of these meditation and visualisation techniques is essential if you wish to reach the level of competence required for morphic field manipulation. Whilst it is possible to get lucky and get to Alpha without using these exercises, our many years of research and thousands of test subjects have proved beyond any doubt that the results are far more consistent, and manifest much more rapidly, when they are used.

As with any exercise regime, best results are obtained when a regular and coherent routine is established. Bingeing on a few days of meditation and then doing nothing for a week or so will achieve very little indeed. It is preferable to do a little, often, than a lot every now and then. Repetition is the key to success.

With that in mind, here is a suggestion for a meditation routine. This assumes you don't already meditate regularly (even if you have done so in the past) and are therefore making a standing start.

Begin by performing the heavy body meditation once per day for a week. You may find the experience so enjoyable that you will be tempted to repeat more than once in any given day, but resist that urge. Remember that these exercises are as much about control as relaxation. You can enter a deep meditation using the heavy body, and you need time between each usage for your brainwaves to return to their regular pattern.

Concurrently to the heavy body, you can start doing the visualisation exercises. You can repeat these several times a day if you want. Do the exercise during the heavy body meditation too, as described earlier. How fast you progress through these exercises will depend on your own ability to visualise. If you have an active imagination you will find it easy, but few people are lucky enough to fall into that category. Don't move onto a new exercise until you are completely comfortable with the one you are working on.

After a week, you can start using the concentration exercises. These can be done two or three times a day if you want. Try and do at least one a day. Don't leave the heavy body exercise behind totally, you should continue to do that once a week. It's like a kind of mental housework, getting everything in order.

You can also start to introduce the countdown meditation. Start slowly, just two or three times in the first week. The next week you can reduce the number of times you do the concentration exercises, and increase the countdown meditation. Over a period of about three weeks, gradually change the balance until you are at a point whereby you do a countdown meditation once a day, and you are no longer using the concentration exercises.

If you follow this as a guide, after a month you will be at the stage where you are doing a heavy body meditation once a week, a countdown meditation daily, and have successfully worked through all of the visualisation exercises. At this point you are now able to enter the Alpha band at will (with the countdown method) and have all the necessary visualisation skills to be able to start on morphic field manipulation. Any time you do a countdown meditation and are not working with morphic fields, use your time at the Alpha band to practice visualising using your own exercises.

Just to reiterate, this is a guide only. If you feel you are making progress more quickly, by all means move ahead when you feel ready. And if you find it tougher and need more practice, that is perfectly okay too and you should extend this to as long as you need. Everyone is unique and comes at this from a different place, there is no one size fits all method, just as there is no single fitness program that will perfectly suit everyone.

THE MANIFESTATION TRIANGLE

You now have the tools to manipulate morphic fields, to ask them to do your bidding, whatever that may be. In the next sections we will look at some specific ways to use the fields—to find love and money—as well as some general advice on how to use them to manifest anything else. But first we must understand what we call the *manifestation triangle*.

The technique of visualisation from a state of Alpha brain-wave frequency is the most direct way we know of to communicate with morphic fields. We are talking to them in their own language, we are on their wavelength (literally!) But this is not enough to get them to work for us. In fact, it is one of three requirements, all of which must be fulfilled in order to see success with morphic fields. The others are *desire* and *belief*. Together, we say that these three ingredients make up the three sides of the manifestation triangle. When all three are present, the triangle is complete. Its like opening a portal through which the morphic fields can manifest your wishes.

Our research and experience has shown us that the best results come when the three sides are present in equal and sufficient measure. However, if one side is lacking, it can be compensated for if the other two sides are stronger. For example, if our technique is not up to scratch, we can still see manifestation of our wishes if our desire and belief are very strong.

We've looked at the technique part already, so let's examine the other sides of the triangle.

Desire

This is the starting point for any use of morphic fields. Without the desire to realise a specific goal, you wouldn't even be reading this book. Not all desires are created equally though. For example, you might think that you want to get back with an ex lover. But do you really? Are you actually suffering, feeling low, because you feel un-loved and unwanted? Would a relationship with someone other than that specific person fulfil your needs? Some-times we think we know what we want, but actually what we truly desire is something different.

This isn't to say that there are some desires that aren't real. Rather, some may be a subset of our true need. In the above example, getting back the ex lover would fulfil our desire for reciprocal love, but would it be the best way to do that? Perhaps, deep down, we know that the relationship was always doomed, that the ex wasn't 'the one', wasn't our soul mate. It can be frightening to admit something like that to ourselves, it means we are going to have to start over, find someone new, begin again. The ex is just easier, a quick fix.

Morphic fields are connected to everything and they *know* everything. This has to be true as they are, by their very nature, present in our brain cells, in our memories. They are part of us. If we try and manipulate them to do some-thing, and that thing isn't what we really, truly want, the fields will know that. There will be a conflict between what we are asking and our true desire.

The problem of course, is how do we know our true desire? We lie to ourselves all the time. We tell ourselves that if we had more money we would be happy. But is it the money that would bring joy, or what the money can buy? Maybe what we *really* want is to be out of debt because that would take away the *fear* of having our house repossessed if we couldn't make the repayments. Sure, manifesting money to pay off the debt would solve the problem and bring happiness, but is it the only way that could happen? What if, for example, a newspaper was running a competition and the prize was "we'll pay off your mortgage"? Winning that competition would achieve the same result, and no money would ever have to enter your bank account or possession. Or maybe another solution would be for someone to offer to buy your house for more than it is worth, enabling you to buy another home without incurring any debt. By focussing on the true desire, the wish to be out of debt, not only do we avoid conflict, we also give the morphic fields much greater scope to find a solution. Whilst they are quite capable of manifesting money, if there is an easier solution to the problem at hand, they will be able to manifest that much more quickly.

So before ever making any attempt at morphic field manipulation, first ask yourself if what you think you want is what you really want. Drill down through the reasons why you are asking for whatever you are. Be brutally honest with yourself. Use a countdown meditation and do the exercise whilst at the Alpha band, you will think more clearly and objectively there. Try and imagine yourself in the future, after whatever you *think* you want, has manifested. If it was money, what did the money buy? And whatever it bought, how has *that* improved your life? That is what you truly desire, not the cash. If it's a person you are trying to obtain, do the same thing. Imagine yourself with that person. Spend some time on this, put in a lot of detail. Will you really be happy, or just be back to a sub-par relationship? Then imagine your ideal partner. If you could create them from thin air, who would they be? How would they spend their time? How would they be with you? You with them? What would they look like? How old would they be? Again, don't be afraid to add detail. Go wild, you're in fantasy land and nobody can see what you're thinking. When you've created this person, compare them to the person you think you want. How do they measure up? Of course, very few people are lucky enough to meet the perfect partner, but if this person is a very long way from your ideal, perhaps you don't really desire them as much as you thought.

Discovering your true desire is vital, but it's not the only part of the equation. You must also maintain that desire. This sounds odd we know. If you want something, you always want it, right? But the stronger you can make your desire, the stronger you make that side of the manifestation triangle, and the better your message will get through to the morphic fields.

Maintaining desire should be easy (if you find it isn't, then go back to step one; you haven't found your true desire!) You should keep it in the back of your mind all the time. When you use the countdown meditation to go to the Alpha band, visualise the outcome of your desire. Make the image as realistic as you can. Use all the senses in your mind's eye. How does it feel when the desire has become reality? What does it look like? Smell like? What can you hear? The more detail you put into your image, the more real it will become to you, and the stronger your desire will be.

Belief

Of the three sides of the triangle, belief is the one that most people have difficulty with. The technique can be learnt and is simply a matter of practise. Desire is a given, with the caveats we have looked at already. But belief can evade even the most open minded.

Why do we even need belief? There is no clear answer to this, but again, testing, research, and thousands of test subjects have proven beyond any doubt whatsoever that the fields work best when we *believe* that they will work. It seems to be the case that our confidence in the process somehow aids the communication of the desire to the morphic fields. If we attempt such communication but don't believe it is really working, we are once again creating a conflict. Our actions say one thing, but our minds are saying quite another. That conflict leaves the third side of the triangle wide open. The circuit isn't closed and so cannot function efficiently.

So what to do, if we fundamentally don't believe the process works? Or if we believe, but have doubts? All is not lost.

The first thing to remember is that the other two sides of the triangle can compensate (up to a point) for a lack of belief. Having a good technique (which comes from repetition of the meditation and visualisation exercises) and a strong, reinforced, true desire, can on their own bring about manifestation. The trouble is that it will take longer if the belief is lacking, and that delay can in itself erode belief!

The single best way to build belief in the process, is to see it work. Of course this is a chicken and egg situation. Building belief can be done by witnessing manifestation, but manifestation requires an element of belief. To get around this, it is best to start by trying to manifest very small easily obtainable things. For example, if you truly desire money (and not what it can buy), it would not be wise to try and manifest a large sum in one go, unless you already had experience of the process and had total confidence in it. Instead, you would start with a very small amount, like ten dollars. When this manifests, you have solid evidence that the process works, and so have a foundation on which to build your belief system. Subsequent uses of the process will boost this every time they manifest. Be cautious of overextending your belief system though. When you have manifested ten dollars, don't then try for ten million! It's too much of a leap in one go, you'll over stretch your confidence in the process to breaking point, not only bringing your belief system crumbling down, but damaging its foundations to the point that you will find it difficult to start over. Slow and steady is the key. Build up your demands of the morphic fields as you build up your confidence in their ability to deliver.

PART TWO - LOVE

INTRODUCTION

In 1943, American psychologist Abraham Maslow published a paper entitled *A Theory of Human Motivation*. The ideas within have become widely accepted throughout the world. The paper suggested that all humans have a hierarchy of needs that must be met in order to achieve happiness. At the lowest level of this hierarchy are basic physiological requirements like breathing, food, water and sleep. Once those are taken care of, our next priority is safety. Physical safety for ourselves and our family, and security too, in terms employment (a lack of which could ultimately affect the ability to meet the lower level needs such as access to food). The next level up from that is love and belonging. So according to Maslow, and many of his peers, once we have made sure we can eat, sleep, and have a roof over our heads to keep us warm, our next highest priority is to find love, friendship, and sexual intimacy.

Little wonder then, that by far the most enquiries we receive in relation to morphic fields and what they can do, stem from relationship problems. Every human being needs to love and to be loved, but it's not always easy to make that happen. On the contrary, it's much tougher than meeting the other, lower level, human needs.

Morphic fields are perfectly suited to helping meet the desire for love. It is not just people who require companionship. Almost every living organism has at least a physical need to reproduce in order to survive, and reproduction generally requires a partner. Morphic fields, bound up as they are in the very fabric of the universe, have what you might call a vested interest in ensuring that happens. Nature has been built in a way that encourages and promotes reproduction, and morphic fields are very much part of that natural design, helping keep the master plan ticking along.

Robert's own experience in morphic fields was born of a desire to revive a broken relationship. When he witnessed first hand the power the morphic fields had in making that happen, it sparked his own research, and ultimately the commercialisation of a method for anyone to tap into the fields themselves for the purposes of getting someone to fall in love with them. Working with customers not only helped those people meet their desires, it also provided a wealth of real life data which was ploughed back into our research. Robert's kit has helped literally thousands of people get back ex lovers, and also start new relationships with people they themselves were in love with, but who didn't have reciprocal feelings.

With this book, you now get to share in all that knowledge. We're going to show you how you too can use the fields to find, or enhance, love. Even if you don't need this process for that particular reason, this section is still worth following along with. The precise techniques we are going to cover apply to most other scenarios you might need morphic fields to resolve.

What Can You Do?

Using this specific process, you can make almost anyone fall in love with you, within reason. The only real limitation is that you must know the person you desire (if you're searching for a soul mate you haven't yet met, you can modify the technique as you will see in Part Four), and they must know who you are. When you do the process, the person you desire will feel a strong and genuine love for you. If they have never seen or met you, then clearly they will have no way of knowing who this love is directed at, or means of acting upon it.

This means, for example, that you cannot use this method on a celebrity, unless you happen to already know them personally. There is nothing to stop you targeting Tom Cruise, or Carey Mulligan, or whoever else you might desire, but when they start feeling emotions for you, they won't know they are for *you*. They will simply feel them as some kind of unrequited, undirected desire. Another reason this will not work on celebrities is that for the process to function, you need very strong desire (one of the sides of the manifestation triangle). Without knowing the person well, it is quite simply not possible to have the necessary level of desire. You might think you are in love with a famous actor or actress, but unless you know them personally, you are really only in love with their public persona, the image they put out there. Anyone who does know somebody in the public eye knows that their private self is usually a very different person to the one we see on the television or in the newspapers. So in the case of celebrity, the desire side of the triangle can never be strong enough, as that desire is for an idea of a person who doesn't really exist.

So who can we direct this process at? Really, just about anyone we know. Most people use this to either get back with an ex-boyfriend, ex-girlfriend, or estranged spouse, or they use it to fulfil an unrequited love, making someone they desire but who doesn't feel the same way about them, fall in love with them.

This is a powerful process, and we urge you to use it responsibly. It is entirely possible to break apart an existing relationship by making one party to that relationship fall deeply in love with you. Certainly that's harder, takes longer, and requires stronger belief and desire, but it can be done. Therefore we encourage anyone who uses this method to consider the consequences of doing so very carefully before they start out.

No pre-existing relationship is necessary for this to work. It functions equally well whether you use it on an ex, or on, for example, a colleague who you desire but who shows no interest in you. It also works regardless of the current feelings of the person you want to use it on. It could be that they like you, but no more than that. It could be that they have no feelings towards you either way. And it can even be (as is often the case when dealing with ex partners) that they actively dislike you, detest you even. We've worked with countless people who have been told by their estranged lover that they never want to see them again at any cost. And yet, when this process is applied, the ex partner softens their stance, starts to warm to their ex, and before long the relationship is rekindled. Usually when this happens, that resulting relationship is even stronger than before.

You can use this process regardless of your sexuality. However, you cannot change the sexuality of the person you are using it on. If you are, for example, a gay man, then you can quite happily and successfully use it on another gay man. It will work exactly the same way as described above. But if you tried it on a straight man, although he would be drawn to you, the most likely outcome is that he would interpret his feelings as friendship and nothing more. Of course, many people believe themselves to be of a particular sexual orientation when in fact they could be suppressing their true desires (sometimes unconsciously), and if that is the case, the process will uncover those desires and the person will feel compelled to act on them. Again though, we ask you to consider the possible consequences when using this method regardless of the situation. Altering someone's feelings is not something to be done lightly.

How Does It Work?

All this talk of making someone fall in love with you can sound quite manipulative. It is natural to be concerned about a method that appears to affect someone's free will, making them do something they otherwise would not do, especially when we are thinking of applying that method to someone we love.

In fact, the process works in a similar way to falling in love naturally. To the person you are 'targeting' (a word which itself sounds manipulative, but which is nonetheless accurate), there is absolutely no difference to the love created by this morphic field process and a love that occurs naturally. Think of it as being like using IVF to get pregnant. All the elements used are the same (sperm, an egg, and a womb), and the resulting baby is no different to any other conceived naturally. IVF just gives nature a helping hand to get things going. This morphic field method uses the same elements as falling in love naturally (the same regions of the brain and the same chemical reactions within those regions), it's just giving nature a push in the right direction.

The physical process by which this works is actually quite simple. You will begin by opening a channel of communication between yourself and the target person, in much the same way Robert and his wife use a channel to pass messages about their shopping requirements. It's a bit like running a telephone cable between your head and their head. With the channel in place, you can actually send your emotion (your love) through the morphic field to the other person. The love is received by the limbic system in their brain in a process scientists call *limbic resonance*. This system deals with a number of higher level brain functions, including emotion. All love is created there, whether it occurs naturally or through limbic resonance. So what's happening is that your love for them is being picked up by their limbic system, and they feel it as their own. In other words they feel it as reciprocal love for you. The love is every bit as real and genuine as if it had occurred naturally (which is essentially to say, by chance). The chemical reactions are the same, the feeling is the same.

Continued use of the morphic field channel will deepen the emotional response, until there comes a point that the person feels compelled to act on it (just as you have felt compelled to act on your own love by starting the process). They will seek you out, try to be with you.

It is not our place to argue the morals or ethics of using this process, that is something anyone considering using it must decide for themselves. In our view, it does not affect free will, as the ultimate decision to act on the love lies with the other person. We believe that so-called 'natural' love occurs randomly by chance, and that the use of this process is no more than giving the dice a nudge so it falls on the side we want. Your view may differ, and is equally valid.

One thing we would ask you to consider though, is the effect on any third party who may be involved. If the person you desire is in a relationship with someone else, that other person will inevitably be affected by the outcome of the process. Morphic fields are a positive force in the universe, and all research shows that they work towards the common good. But our experience has proven to us time and again that they are perfectly capable of breaking apart an existing relationship. They won't do this directly. You couldn't use this process just to split up a relationship out of spite, for example. A breakup can however, be a by-product of the person you desire falling in love with you.

Again, this is an ethical decision that you alone can make. Relationships fall apart every day, and perhaps you believe the relationship the target is currently in is destined to be one of them. Perhaps you are simply provoking the inevitable. Only you know the answer, and only you can decide.

How Long Does It Take?

It is important to understand that this method will not instigate an overnight change in someone. If you start using it today, you are not going to wake up tomorrow to find the person of your dreams banging on your door desperate to see you. It is very much a gradual process that takes some weeks or even months.

Planting emotions in the limbic system of another person is like planting a seed in the garden. They need time to take root and grow. And just as some gardens are filled with rich, fertile soil, have just the right amount of sun, shade, and water, and so see their seeds grow quickly and strongly, some people have more fertile minds. If your planted emotion finds a mind that is already predisposed to love, and to you, then you will see results much more quickly than if it is sown in a closed mind that has shut out the idea of love or happiness, or of you.

Every person and every mind on the planet is entirely unique. For that reason, it is impossible to predict before starting this method, just how long it will take to see it through to fruition. If your desire is strong enough though, this will not be a problem, you will have the motivation to keep going.

Because the effect of the process occurs entirely within the brain (and therefore the mind) of the person you are using it on, you will rarely be able to see any evidence of that effect until they choose to act on it. They can begin to have feelings for you right from the very first day you begin, but they are no more likely to fling themselves into your arms as you would be to throw yourself at someone you suddenly developed an interest in. Instead, the emotions will take hold, develop, and grow. Sometimes, particularly in the case of doing this on an ex partner, the person can appear to distance themselves from you for a time. If they previously had negative feelings towards you and then suddenly and inexplicably find themselves developing conflicting emotions, that conflict can naturally cause a kind of withdrawal. It's like if you went to stroke a cute fluffy little dog and the dog turned round and bit your hand. Your initial feeling ("cute, fluffy, sweet!") draws you to stroke the animal, and the shock of him biting you causes you to pull away. Or to take a different example, you may hold a particular political view, and someone starts debating a counter argument with you. Your natural response will probably be to dig your heels in and argue your case more strongly. But if the other argument makes much more sense, you may eventually come round to their way of thinking. Our brains are built in a way that they naturally defend what they believe to be true, the status quo. So when your ex lover, who believes they never want to see you again, begins to feel attraction towards you, their brain will rebel, dig in, and fight off those feelings. That can manifest itself through them avoiding contact with you, or even actively telling you they don't want to see you again, or in any other number of ways. Although this can be distressing, it is always a sign that the morphic field channel is strong and that the emotions are taking route. Further use of the process will see them grow to the point that they will accept them and embrace them. Ultimately they will become so all-consuming, the person will take some kind of positive action, such as contacting you. We call this *externalisation*, it is the point at which the internal effect of the emotion is made external through actions. More often than not it can seem like nothing is happening for days, weeks, or even months, and then one day the person suddenly calls you up and declares their undying love. It can appear like a switch has been flipped in their head. But of course the reality is that those feelings have been growing steadily all the time, hidden from your view, until the point of externalisation.

How Long Does It Last?

There are two questions we are asked about this process more often than any other. The first is "Will this work in my situation?" The answer to that one is always yes, unless the situation is that it is to be used on a celebrity, or someone of a different sexual preference to the person asking the question. The second most common question is "How long will it last? Can I make them love me forever?" The answer to that is no, you cannot force someone to love you forever.

As we have seen, the morphic field process creates the emotion of love in the limbic system of the person it is directed at. This is exactly the same as if that love occurred naturally by chance. Because it is the identical emotion, it works in precisely the same way. Just as a baby conceived through IVF has no physical or mental attributes different to a baby conceived naturally, and is is certainly not immortal, so a love created by this method has no more reason to last any longer than a love that occurs by chance.

Love can be a fragile emotion. A relationship requires nurture and care. If it is not nourished and looked after it will wither and die, just like the plant in the garden that is not watered and is deprived of sunlight.

Having said that, if you use the process to help someone fall in love with you, then enjoy a loving and happy relationship with them, and that relationship begins to turn sour, there is no reason you cannot reuse the process to give it a helping hand. When someone already has love for you, the process works very easily indeed. It can nurse the love back to full health rather than having to plant a new seed and wait for it to grow.

Prerequisites

Now that we know the limitations of the process, let's take a look at exactly what it involves. The first thing you will need is a picture of the person you desire. No doubt they already fill your head every waking moment, but a picture will help focus your mind. Any kind of picture will do, it could be a regular old fashioned photograph print, or something you printed yourself, or a picture on a screen such as a computer, tablet, or phone. All will work just fine. Similarly, it doesn't matter if there are other people in the picture as well.

The sole purpose of the picture is to focus your thoughts and enhance your desire. You will spend a few minutes looking at it before entering the Alpha band through meditation. Later you will be visualising the person you desire, so filling your mind with their image beforehand will really help with this. It also helps enhance your desire, one of the three sides of the manifestation triangle. You can proceed without using a photograph, but in thousands of test subjects we have consistently seen better results when a picture is used.

Next up, you will need to to find something that the other person has touched. It does *not* have to be anything they own or have previously owned, they just need to have touched it at some point in the past. It can be quite literally anything. An item of clothing, a pen, a phone, a book, a mug, really anything at all. It doesn't matter if the thing you choose has been washed or cleaned since it was touched, it will be fit for the purpose.

And what is the purpose of this article? It is there mainly to assist in the belief side of the triangle. Keeping close by an article that has a physical association with the desired person, no matter how tenuous that link might be, helps the mind get to grips with the process. When we are visualising at Alpha, it is the right side—the creative side—of our brain that is doing all the work. The logic-loving left side has nothing to do, and can end up trying to sabotage our efforts. Any lack of belief in the process will come from the left side. By giving it something to hang onto, we keep the left side happy. We can think of this article as being a sort of mental crutch, a stick to prop up the weaker part of the mind.

It's not just about tricking our brain though. There is evidence that every physical interaction we have with another object, leaves a trace behind in the morphic field. Our touched item then, also works as a kind of GPS. It has a link back to that person, and so can provide information to the field about them and how to find them.

Now that you have all the articles required, you are almost ready to begin the process. However, before you do so for the first time, there is one more preparatory step to take. You need to think of a scene in your head, in which you and the person you desire are together and as happy as you can imagine. If you are doing this to get back with an ex partner, the scene can be one from the past, when you were already together (but it doesn't have to be, you can use an imagined scene if you prefer.) If you are using this method to get together with someone you haven't previously been in a relationship with, you will need to invent a scene from scratch. Think about a particular moment when you will be together, how you will feel to be with this person. As always when we are visualising, the more detail you can add the better. Think about where the scene takes place. Is it inside or out? What is the weather like? Are there other people around? What sounds can you hear? How is the other person reacting? We call this scene our *moment of perfection.* You will need to call upon it every time you use the process, so it is worth investing some time up front to make it as great as you can. When creating it for the first time, you may want to be at the Alpha band in a meditation. Your imagination is on peak form when at Alpha. From which point of view you picture the scene is your choice. Most people naturally see it as if they are themselves in the scene, looking out through their own eyes. But some people prefer to see it from the outside looking in, as if they are watching themselves. Either way is fine, you should use whichever comes naturally to you.

Method

You are now ready to begin the process proper. Start by finding a comfortable position, somewhere you will not be disturbed. This is even more important than when you are simply practising as you will be opening a connection to the other person, and any interference can disturb that. It won't stop the process working, but it can most certainly slow it down. You will need to allow up to fifteen minutes for the meditation.

The first step is to spend a few moments looking at the picture of the person you desire (from here on in we will refer to them, as the *target*, with the usual caveat that despite the nature of the word, a target is not someone we are manipulating.) Fill your mind with their image. When you feel ready, put the picture down somewhere nearby, and make sure you have the article they touched nearby as well.

To enter the Alpha bad for morphic field manipulation work, we always use the countdown method. If you have worked through the exercises discussed in the previous section, it will be the most efficient and consistent way to reach the correct level. If you downloaded a harmonic Alpha audio track from our Resources page, use that too.

When you have reached the Alpha band, you should call to mind your moment of perfection. Spend a few minutes on this, it is what is creating a link between you and the target. What is happening at the Alpha level is you are bringing about a resonance between yourself and the target. They won't feel this, it happens on a totally subconscious level.

The next step is about using the link to send your love to their limbic system. To do this, you need to isolate the target person. In your mind's eye, dissolve the scene you are looking at, with the exception of the target, and, if you are looking at this from a third party point of view perspective (i.e. you can see yourself), yourself. In other words, your image is now entirely blank with the exception of the target, and possibly yourself if you are looking in from the outside. Put yourself next to the target, facing them. You should now either be looking directly at them, or you will be looking at yourself and the target facing each other. You are standing about a metre apart (or a yard in old money).

Between the two of you, imagine a small ball of light, about the size of a tennis ball. It will be hovering above the ground, at about waist height. The light ball glows a soft yellow. You and the target look at the ball. As you watch, it starts to grow larger.

Within yourself, call to mind the love that you have for the target. From your moment of perfection you should already be feeling this desire. Being it to the fore, feel it flow through your body. As you do so, the ball of light between you is growing. Not so big that it touches you yet, but nearly. Keep focussing on your love for this person. Look into their eyes, feel them looking at you. They desire you as much as you desire them. Intensify your emotion until you feel ready to burst. Imagine that all the love inside of you is binding together into a ball of energy. You might feel it in your stomach or your chest. Gather it together, feed it. Now you must expel the ball of energy inside you. Feel it propel itself out of your body and hurl itself into the ball of yellow light. As it joins the light, it combines with it, growing it much bigger. The ball becomes so large that it is now touching you and the target. You can feel its energy as it does so. It keeps on growing until you are now both standing inside it. It feels warm and full of love. You feel safe, and fully connected to this person you so desire. Hold onto that feeling for as long as you can, up to about a minute if possible (don't worry about being precise with times here, it is difficult to judge time in Alpha. Just hold it until it feels right.)

Finally, you will slowly dissolve the image in your mind. Empty your mind's eye so that you see nothing, only blackness or white. You can then count yourself out using the count up script.

When you have finished, you may feel exhausted, or exhilarated. Or you might feel nothing at all. There is no correct way you must feel when you are done. You will probably wonder 'did it work?' which is a natural question to ask yourself. If you followed the steps and were at Alpha, then you can rest assured that it will have worked.

You're not done yet though. This was one time thorough the process. You will need to do more. In fact there is a schedule of repetition you should follow. This schedule hasn't come about randomly. Like everything else in this book, it is the result of many years of research and development, and the combined experience of thousands of test subjects.

We use a schedule of repetition because it is important to keep up the emotional energy in the target's limbic system. Every time you go through the process, you increase that energy level, reinforcing the emotional response within them. However, it is equally important not to overdo things. We have already discussed how the initial reaction of the target person can be withdrawal due to sudden and unexpected emotions and the conflict that causes. Putting in too much energy too quickly can send that conflict right over the edge, actually driving them away permanently. The key is to strike a balance between keeping up the emotional pressure, without putting in so much that it explodes out of control. The schedule we present here has been shown time and again to provide an optimum balance.

You will start by doing the process one time a day for three consecutive days. These three days will establish a strong link between yourself and the target. After the last of these three days, you should stop for one week. You can continue to practise meditations, but do not do the above process. This week long break gives the emotions you have planted, time to take root.

After the week has elapsed (you can wait a few days longer if necessary) you can start what we call the *reinforcing procedure*. You simply redo the process one time per day, every two days, for one week. In other words, four times in all. This procedure feeds the emotion in the limbic system of the target, making it grow stronger. It is possible, though unlikely, that you start to see some early signs of externalisation at this point. If you don't, don't panic. It is unusual to see such signs this soon. Rest assured that beneath the surface, inside their head, it is all bubbling away.

After the reinforcing procedure, you take another break. This time it is for two weeks (fourteen days). Again, you can extend this if necessary (if you are away on vacation or otherwise engaged for example). This can be a very difficult period because you will feel as though you are not doing anything, that you should be taking more positive action. But actually this is the most positive, helpful action you can take. Like the seed in the garden, the love needs time to grow. Feed it too much and you will just end up killing it.

What you have done to this point, we call a single *round* of the procedure. This round starts from the first day of the process, and finishes at the end of the two week waiting period. So after the two week period has elapsed, you have performed one complete round of the procedure. You're still not done yet though! You should always do at least two rounds. So after the two week waiting time is over, you will effectively start again, doing a procedure once a day for three days, then waiting a week, then doing a reinforcing procedure week, and then waiting two weeks.

Again, you may start to see externalisation during this second round. Even if that happens, and even if you see full manifestation (i.e. you are now with the target person in a full loving relationship), you should complete the second round regardless.

If no externalisation is evident, after the two week wait you can start a third round. In fact there is no upper limit on the number of rounds you can perform. The only rules are that you should do a minimum of two, and if you start a round, you must always finish it.

When you perform the procedure, it doesn't matter if you do so during the day or at night. Some people report a slightly faster result if they do this when the target person is sleeping, but the difference is negligible and certainly not worth putting yourself to additional trouble for. If it is easier to do this during the day, then definitely do it during the day.

What is more important is to try and perform the procedure at around the same time each day. Try and get to within one hour of the same time. So if, for example, on day one you start at 9am, on day two you should attempt to start between 8am and 10am. And on day three, you should start within an hour of whatever time you started day two. For the reinforcing procedure the clock resets and you can start day one at any time you like, but days two three and four should be within an hour each way of that time. Any subsequent rounds you perform, the clock resets again.

Doing the procedure at around the same time each day keeps the twenty four hour separation required to prevent any emotional overload. If you started at 10pm one day and then the next day started at 8am, you would only have left fourteen hours, which is not sufficient time for the emotions to settle in the target's limbic system.

With the best will in the world, sometimes it is not possible to prevent being disturbed during the procedure. If this happens, you should stop your meditation (counting yourself out if possible). If the interruption occurred before you imagined the ball of light between you, then you should wait half an hour or so (to make sure your brainwave frequency has fully returned to the Beta band), and then restart that day. If it was after the ball of light, you should abandon the day, but count it as complete. For example, if you were disturbed on day two and had already started the ball of light phase, you would stop and then carry on on day three as if day two had been completed.

If you somehow miscount the days and perform the procedure too often, you should stop and wait for a minimum of twenty one days before starting the round over again. This twenty one day period will allow the emotions in the limbic system to die back to a level where we can be sure that additional procedures will not cause an overload.

What Happens Next

Performing the procedure is the easy part. Waiting to see externalisation is much harder. There will almost certainly be times when you question whether or not it is working. The situation may even appear to get worse for a while, for the reasons we have already looked at. The key to surviving this waiting time is to try not to focus on the process at all. Don't analyse everything the other person does or says. It can be tempting to examine every move they make, to try and figure out what it means, but actually it means very little or nothing at all.

The process has a push-pull effect. It can be a case of two steps forward and one step back. You may see sudden and marked changes in the target, they may appear to be making advances. But those advances can just as quickly turn around, and you see them back off, keep their distance, even tell you to stay away. This is all perfectly normal behaviour as they grapple with their newfound emotions. Ultimately they will come around. Analysing every step along that path though, will simply lead to frustration and anxiety.

In some cases you won't see any push-pull type effect. Indeed you may see nothing at all. You will begin to wonder if the process has worked, or it if is doing anything. This is the hardest thing to deal with. At least if they change their behaviour towards you, you have some evidence that the process is having an emotional effect on them. When you see nothing, it is easy to imagine that this means nothing is occurring, which again leads to frustration and worry.

Not only is such frustration unpleasant for you to deal with, it can actually slow down the process. Remember, from the moment you perform the very first meditation in the process, you are connected to the target person. They will become sensitive to your emotions. The love you send is transmitted clearly and directly to them while you are in the Alpha band using the visualisation, but even outside that time, they will sense very strong feelings that you have. If you allow those thoughts and feelings to become deeply negative and dominant, it is inevitable that they will pick up on them. Just as their limbic system will experience your love and interpret it as their own, so it will detect your negativity. This usually won't stop the process working entirely, after all, you won't be sending directed negativity in the same way you send tightly focussed love. But it can be enough to tip the balance out of your favour and thus slow down progress, or cause the target person to pull back a little. The danger, of course, is that this slowing down will bring about more negative feelings and despondency in you, and a vicious circle ensues.

Avoiding these unhealthy thoughts and feelings can be tough at times, but is by no means impossible. As with everything else, it requires some practice. The single best way to avoid this kind of negative thinking is to become aware of what you are thinking. It sounds obvious, but actually most of the time we let our minds wander wherever they want, and we pay no attention to our thoughts. To keep negative ideas from taking hold in your mind, you must become a policeman (or policewoman) of your head. You must get into the habit of *noticing* every time you think something negative. This isn't something you can do actively, there is no switch in the brain that you can flick on to have it alert you of undesirable musings. It has to be formed as a habit. When you notice yourself thinking something negative, stop and make a big deal out of it. Tell yourself that these kinds of thoughts are not healthy and that they must be avoided, and then make an effort to change them by thinking of something positive. If you can't think of anything positive, just think of something different. Open a book, put on the television or radio, go out and do something, or concentrate on your work. Just make a decisive effort to move your thinking away from the negativity.

You won't catch every bad thought this way, but the more you do notice, the better you will get at noticing them. If you can, try and keep score. Each time you find yourself thinking in a direction you shouldn't be, chalk it up somewhere. Not only will you likely be surprised by how many you catch in a day, but you'll also be able to see your progress as you catch fewer and fewer.

Policing your thoughts is essential, but clearly the best solution is to avoid negative emotions altogether. Many will arise naturally from your anxiousness surrounding the procedure. To keep these ideas at bay, try and occupy your mind with other things as much of the time as possible. Crowd out negative, ideas, don't give them room to take hold and grow. Throw yourself into your work. Start a new project in the garden. Learn a new language. Take up evening classes. Redecorate a room. Do something completely detached from the target person, something positive that you enjoy. Not only will it leave little or no space for unwanted images to make their way into your head, but when they do occasionally get through, you will have something new to think about to replace them with.

If it is possible to do so, you should try and remain in contact with the target. This will make it easier for them to act on their feelings when the time comes. If they have to go to some effort to find you and declare their love for you, they will. But they'll usually do it sooner if you are right there. However, this comes with a big caveat. It is important not to change your behaviour towards this person. If you never ever talk to them, don't suddenly start doing so now. There are two reasons for this. The first is that your change in how you approach them combined with the emotions that they start to feel from the process, will combine, and may be too much to deal with in one go. The second reason is that if you change the way you behave in order to try and help the process, that is a subtle indication to your subconscious mind that you don't have enough confidence in the process to do its job. This will weaken the belief side of the manifestation triangle—a side which is most likely already the weakest.

Remaining consistent to your behaviour isn't limited to contact with the target, it applies to everything else surrounding them. If, for example, you always meet up with them for a coffee on Wednesdays, keep doing that. Don't change how you dress, or the kinds of things you say or do. Don't decide to move house to be nearer to them. If you find yourself thinking "I wonder if what I am about to do will affect the process?", the answer is always the same—do whatever you would do if there was no process. That way you won't be changing your behaviour, you won't confuse the message, and you won't erode your own belief.

The same applies to making a move on the target. It can be tempting to jump the gun and declare your feelings for them before you have seen any sign of externalisation. This is never advisable for all the same reasons. They will have enough going on in their heads, and will need space to deal with that. When the time is right, they'll come to you.

After starting this process, you may find yourself thinking even more about the other person, and you might experience vivid dreams, even if you rarely dream. This is not at all uncommon. It happens due to *emotional feedback* through the morphic field channel. Your own limbic system is picking up echoes of the emotions you have sent across it, and possibly even the target's own thoughts being transmitted back to you. If it happens, it is a great sign as it means you have a strong and healthy channel. Don't worry if it doesn't happen, it's not a sign you didn't make the channel strong enough. It is simply the case that not all people produce the echo effect.

Finally, remember that even when you begin to see externalisation, and even full manifestation of their newfound love for you, if you have started a round you should complete it.

PART THREE - MONEY

INTRODUCTION

Earlier in the book when we looked at the *desire* side of the manifestation triangle, we investigated how important it is to find our true desire, not what we think—superficially—we want. Money is often cited as the single thing that would make the most difference to happiness and contentment. Yet money doesn't appear in Maslow's hierarchy of needs. Instead we have security. Security from the elements for ourselves and our families, by means of a roof over our heads. Security from hunger, by having a cupboard full of food. And security from health problems by being clothed, fed, and looked after by medical professionals when the need arises. Money—currency, or cash in the bank—is no more than a proxy for the security that we really crave. It is also a proxy for other material goods that we believe will make us happier. It could be a new car, a shiny iPad, a Picasso, or three weeks a year somewhere sunny near the sea. All of these end goals are the real desires, not the bits of paper with numbers printed on them that allow us to purchase these goods.

Having said that, people still choose to believe that money is what they really want. It provides access to the security and goods that we actually need, and it also provides the freedom to obtain them as and when we feel like it. It is for this reason (in part) that we include here a section on how to use the morphic field process to manifest money.

We also chose to include this section because money is something virtually everyone who will ever read this book could use more of. Even multimillionaire footballers, bankers and businessmen look to obtain more money. So this section provides a great example to follow along with. Once you have understood how the process works to manifest money (and love, if you used that process as well), you will have all the tools you need to adapt it to manifest anything else you want.

Morphic fields are probably responsible for more wealth generation than anything else. Sadly they are rarely given the credit they are due. This is perhaps not surprising, the field of research is young.

Back in the late 1930s, Napoleon Hill wrote what was to become a classic book on wealth generation (actually it's about much more than that, but if you take it simply at face value, it's about obtaining money). It was called *Think And Grow Rich*. The techniques within have been used by countless people over many generations to build businesses and amass huge wealth. If you boil down the methods Hill teaches, distill their essence, you see that actually they are all about morphic field manipulation. The only reason he never mentions these fields by name is that science hadn't caught up with his own research by the time his book was published

Hill's techniques are good and they work, but they are a little dated. The process we use, and that you will learn, is every bit as powerful (arguably more so) but much easier to implement, and more efficient. That's because we have the benefit of scientific research to tell us how to manipulate the fields effectively. Think And Grow Rich is the proverbial sledgehammer to crack a nut. What we're showing you is how to use a precision laser to split it cleanly open instead.

What Can You Do?

There is no theoretical limit to the amount of money you can attract using this process. In reality though, you are restricted by the strength of your manifestation triangle.

The desire side of the triangle will be tempered by the fact you probably don't truly desire the money, rather, what you can buy with it.

The real limiting factor for you though, is probably going to be the belief side. Human beings are naturally skeptical creatures, we like to see proof. We are back at the chicken and egg situation of wanting proof in order to believe, and having to believe in order to see proof.

As we have already suggested, the way around this is to start small. Make your first use of the process be for a small and very specific amount.. When this comes into your possession, use that success to boost your reserves of belief and then start over for a slightly larger amount. Don't try for a million dollars (or a million of anything) straight off, or you will be disappointed and will adversely affect your belief system. By all means build up to it though. Build on each little success as if you were building a stairway. One step at a time will get you to your lofty goal more quickly than you think.

How Does It Work?

In Part Two we saw how you can create love within another person by connecting to them through morphic fields. Obtaining money works in exactly the same way, except instead of connecting to a person, we are connecting to wealth. There is one significant difference though. When we connect to a person we desire, we connect to that specific person (obviously). When we connect to money, or wealth, we do not specify a source of that wealth. To do so would be to artificially limit the possible means by which the wealth could come into our possession.

For example, if you were to try and obtain a million dollars by winning the lottery, the morphic fields would have their work cut out. They would need to influence the numbered balls that come out of the machine for a draw, and they would also need to influence potentially hundreds of people who might choose those same numbers on the same week as you, in order to ensure that they chose something else, thus ensuring the jackpot wasn't shared too thinly. With enough desire and belief, this would no doubt be possible, but far from easy. But what if someone decided they really needed to buy your home, and they would pay any price for it? Perhaps that would be another way a million dollars could come into your possession. Or maybe you could have an idea for a killer product or service. You might not have to develop the idea very far before a rich investor came along and offered to buy you out. This sort of thing happens all the time (far more often than we ever read about in newspapers or online). Perhaps a start up company will decide they absolutely must have you working for them, and they will offer you a million dollar contract. Or a talent scout could spot you in the street and decide you are the face they've been looking for to launch a new campaign, a campaign that has a multi-million dollar budget.

A million dollars is a lot of money and yet even for such a sum, it's easy to quickly come up with a variety of ways it could come into your possession. For smaller amounts that number of ways grows exponentially. Any one of those ways may individually be more unlikely than winning the lottery, but you only need one of them to happen to acquire the sum you are looking for. If you were to direct morphic field energy at only the lottery, you would be shutting off that multitude of other avenues, making the job much harder. If, on the other hand, you were to direct the morphic fields to go out and *find* a million dollars for you, then they would have a world of potential open to them.

The difference is like walking into a town and saying: "I'm thirsty, I need to buy a bottle of Evian water from a Boots pharmacy." You might be able to find a Boots pharmacy, and they may stock Evian, but if you close yourself to other opportunities for water, you could end up visiting a few towns before you get to drink. If you widened your search and said: "I need to get a drink of water," then you would have a much easier time. Half the shops in town could likely oblige, along with all the cafes, bars, take aways, restaurants, drinking fountains, and probably a fair number of accommodating locals.

So the first rule when it comes to acquiring money, or almost anything else non-specific, is to be open minded about where it can come from, to not shut off possible sources, even those you might never have thought of. To do this, we try to connect to the money itself. That way we are sending a message out to the morphic fields saying: "I want this *amount* of money," rather than saying: "I want this *actual* money".

The morphic fields are naturally efficient. Like water flowing down hill, they will find the path of least resistance between us and the money we desire. We don't need to know where that money is, or the path the fields are taking, in order for the connection to be made.

Now of course, money doesn't have a limbic system into which we can plant emotions, as we do when using the process for love. But neither does it exist in a vacuum. Money is controlled by people, and morphic field energy can influence those people in the same way. Even without the intervention of people, the fields can directly influence matter itself, as all matter is inherently connected to them. The combined force of direct attraction of the money itself, and the influence of those controlling it, is powerful indeed.

How Long Does It Take?

Manifestation of money will usually take longer the greater the amount you try and obtain. This is in part down to the strength of the belief side of the triangle. Higher amounts generally (in our experience with clients) come with less belief. There is no logical reason for this. Why should we find it easier to accept that the fields can bring us a hundred dollars than a million? The answer is that we have been conditioned through our lives to think that money is difficult to obtain, and that the larger the sum, the more difficult it is. Money is deeply associated with work (particularly in western culture), so it goes against our programmed instinct to try and imagine that there is absolutely no more work involved in obtaining a six or seven figure sum than one with fewer zeros. This is why we must prime the belief system by obtaining smaller amounts to start with.

Of course, there are also logistical reasons why higher amounts take longer to manifest, and those we have already discussed. There are simply fewer places from where large sums can come. The fields have limited options, and may well have to look further afield to bring you the cash.

To try and put a timescale on all this, in our experience, smaller amounts (under a hundred dollars) can manifest in anything from a week to a month or more, depending on the strength of the manifestation triangle of the person doing the process. If that same person, having manifested this small sum, subsequently goes on to try and obtain four figures, they typically see results in the same kind of time frame. Their belief system has been ratcheted up a notch. If they were to miss out the smaller amount though, and start immediately with a number somewhere between one and ten thousand dollars, then manifestation usually takes more than three months. So as you can see, it really is worth starting small and working up. Ir provides quicker results overall.

Prerequisites

Just like in the love process, you are going to use a detailed visualisation which you will perform whilst in the Alpha band. So before starting, the first step is to build this visualisation.

When you have settled on an exact figure for how much money you are trying to obtain, you must decide what you are going to do with it, even if it is simply to put it into the bank and admire the figure on your monthly statement. The use to which you will put this money should be something that excites you and motivates you, thus building up the desire side of the manifestation triangle. Even if you are going to be using it to pay off the electricity bill (not the most exciting thing in the world) there is a positive element to this; you will have no more debt to the electricity company, you will be free from worries about having the power to your home cut off. That positive outcome is the thing you must focus on, more than the money itself.

The image you build for use in the procedure requires three elements:

1) You
2) The outcome
3) The money

You don't have to see yourself in the image, you could be observing it from your own point of view. But that point of view must allow for you to be *there*, not watching from afar as if you were watching a film. In other words, if you set your visualisation in your living room, you could either see yourself in that room, or see the living room from the point of view of you being there (looking out through your own eyes). Either way is fine, provided you implicate yourself in the image.

In this image you will be celebrating the outcome of what-ever it is you did with the money. If you put it in the bank, you could be looking at a bank statement, or an online balance, showing the cash in your account. If you used it to buy something, try and get that something into the im-age.

The money must also be present, even if you would al-ready have spent it in order to obtain the outcome. You might choose to represent it in cash terms—literally a pile of bills—for a smaller amount, or you might want to im-agine a cheque, or even a line on a bank statement.

When you have decided on the framework for your image (the location where it is set, your point of view, the money and the outcome), you can then start to fill in the detail. The more you can add, the better the process will work. Remember to use all five senses here. What sounds can you hear? What smells are there? Are you sitting? Stand-ing? On what? Is there anyone else around? What are they saying? Doing? Is it hot or cold? What else is going on around you? You're building up a picture here, and you want to make it as realistic as possible.

By far the most important element though, is how you *feel* in the visualisation. Your pleasure, your joy, or your release from having this money should be palpable. It is this emotion that is going to get the morphic fields fired up and working for you, so the stronger you can make it the better.

Spend as much time as you need on this image creation. Make it memorable, you're going to be using it regularly during the procedure.

In order to help strengthen the belief side of the mani-festation triangle, you can once again use some mental crutches to occupy the logical left side of your brain. The first of these is very simply a piece of paper on which you have written the precise figure of how much money you are trying to obtain. The paper should have nothing else on it.

The second crutch is a candle, and it is optional. Our research shows a higher rate of success when the candle is used. It provides a strong focal point for the mind, but there is no evidence that it in any way enhances or helps the morphic fields themselves. If you choose to use a candle, then any variety is fine. Scented candles can work, provided the scent is not so strong as to put you off the task in hand (some can be quite overpowering!) Write onto the side of the candle the figure for the money you wish to obtain. A ballpoint pen is usually good for this, but you can use any writing implement. Finally, ensure that the candle is well secured and safe. You'll have your eyes closed while it is lit, and you obviously do not want any accidents involving a flame.

METHOD

The method itself is very similar to that we looked at for the love process. You will start by finding a comfortable position somewhere you will not be disturbed. Allow fifteen minutes for the meditation. Although it will probably be done more quickly is is always preferable to leave a little leeway. Before you begin, remind yourself of the exact figure you are trying to obtain.

Light the candle, and make sure it is safe and secure.

When you are ready, close your eyes, take a deep breath and let it out slowly. Use the countdown method to enter the Alpha band.

Once in Alpha, empty your mind's eye. Everything should be blank, no images and no sounds. It could be that all around you is white, or black, it doesn't matter as long as it is completely empty, a void. Now imagine a number floating in front of you. The number is the amount of money you desire. You can make this number any colour and dimension you want, but it should be just out of your reach.

Now visualise a small white ball of light floating in the air between you and the number. It is at about your shoulder height, and glows brightly. Watch it slowly grow bigger and bigger. As it does so, try and feel your desire for the money grow deeper. When the ball of light has grown so much that it is almost touching you and the floating number, gather up all your desire and feel it force its way out of you and into the ball. As it joins with it, the ball grows massively in size, enveloping you and the number. It is like an explosion of white, and for an instant you can see nothing, so blinding is the light.

Your eyes slowly adjust, and as they do, you picture the visualisation that you have prepared in advance. Make it as rich and detailed as you can, and really experience the feeling of having already obtained the money. Bask in the glow of that feeling for a few minutes if you can. Let it wash over you and fill you up.

When you are ready, fade the image in your mind's eye to white, and then use the count out script to come back out of the Alpha band. Extinguish the candle, and you are done for the meditation.

It may be the case that the candle went out while you had your eyes closed. This isn't a problem, and there is no need to re-do the day's meditation if it happens. The candle is there to assist your brain during the procedure, and as you weren't aware it had gone out at the time, it did its job regardless.

As with the love procedure, one meditation is not going to be enough to manifest the money that you want. That first run through has sent the morphic field energy off to search for the money you are looking for. You'll need to do it multiple times to ensure a strong link is made, and to use that link to attract the cash. Unlike the love procedure, there is no danger of overloading anyone's emotions, so there is more flexibility in the repetitions. You should still be wary though. If you repeat too often, the process can become almost automatic, you'll just be going through the motions. Every time you do it you need to really *feel* the sense of having obtained the money, and feel the sensation of what that means. It's harder to do that if you're mind isn't really on it because you're just running on auto pilot.

We recommend that you repeat the procedure once a day for three consecutive days. Again, try and be within an hour of the same time each day, thus ensuring the meditations are evenly spaced. There is no reinforcing required, you simple repeat the 'round' of three days the following week, or later if you cannot make it precisely one week.

If the candle burns out before the money has manifested, you can replace it with a new one. There's no need to do so just because the numbers you wrote on are no longer visible, only when there's not enough left to burn for the duration of a meditation. If you do need a new candle, it doesn't have to be the same as the previous one. You just need to be able to write the sum of money on the side.

Unlike when using this method for love, there is no requirement to finish every round you start. If you begin a new week and then the money comes into your possession, there is no need to perform the other meditations in that week.

What Happens Next

Between rounds, you should keep a positive outlook and not think about or worry about the process. If you're just doing this to have extra money for something nice, this should be fairly easy. It can be more difficult if you really desperately need the money quickly though. All the comments from Part Two of the book apply equally here. Keep busy, police your thoughts, and don't dwell on negativity. Such undesirable thoughts won't push the money away from you in the same way they can push away a person you desire, but they can send mixed messages to the morphic fields. Over time that can weaken the link they are creating between you and the money, slowing down progress.

Try not to second-guess how the money is going to come to you. You might think that you know, but you don't. Even if something happens to suggest it is going to manifest by one particular means, keep your mind open to others, because until it is in your possession, anything can happen. Our clients who use this process constantly tell us of their amazement at the diverse, unusual, or unexpected sources of cash, even when they have already used the process on multiple occasions.

If you find yourself being drawn to do something, especially something you might not normally do, go with the flow and see where it takes you. It could be, for example, you feel a sudden and unexpected urge to go and visit a library, or explore a neighbouring town, or even just go for a walk somewhere. Whatever the urge might be, if at all possible, act on it. The morphic fields will try and draw the money to you, but they may also draw you to the money. Getting you to meet it in the middle could well be the most efficient means of bringing you together. Remember, don't try and predict where these urges will take you or the outcome they could have. Just let them show you the way, and enjoy the ride.

Clearly you will know when you acquire the money. You will also know that it was the morphic fields responsible, because the amount will be the same or very close to the figure you chose. If it's not precisely what you were trying for, it will usually be slightly more. It seems morphic fields prefer to over deliver!

Once you have the money, you can start the process over for a new amount. Use your success to boost your belief system. Before each subsequent meditation (be it for money or anything else), bring to mind this success. Remind yourself how well the process worked. Get yourself pumped up about your ability to use the morphic fields.

PART FOUR - ANY OTHER BUSINESS

MAKE IT YOUR OWN

So far you've seen in detail how you can use the meditations and visualisations at the Alpha brainwave band to manipulate morphic field energy in order to attract love and money into your life. The concepts and the methods you have learnt can be used for so much more. Almost anything that you desire can be attracted to you through the use of morphic fields. All you need to do is create a 'recipe' for manifestation, like the recipes that we have provided you here. Your recipe should contain these ingredients:

Mental Crutch. Something the logical left hand side of your brain can grab onto. It can be as simple as a piece of paper with your desire written on it. The more meaningful—to you—that the object you choose is, the better it will work for you. If it can have some kind of physical link to whatever it is you want (like the object touched by the person you desire in Part Two), then that's even better because the morphic fields will use that connection as well. You may wish to include a candle too. It isn't essential, but a lot of people do better when one is present. If your belief system is up to the job, you can dispense with the crutch altogether, but we wouldn't recommend it until you have considerable experience and a good amount of success behind you. Your mental crutch supports the belief side of the manifestation triangle.

A Strong Image. Like the image we built up in Part Three, your mental picture should set the scene for how things will be once you have acquired whatever it is you desire. This is the end goal, and is the grand finale of your visualisation at the Alpha band. The image should be as detailed as you can make it, and should invoke as many of your five senses as possible. The more senses you use, the more areas of your brain you will light up, and the stronger the signal you will send to the morphic fields. And the better your image, the greater the level of desire you will create within yourself, taking care of another of the triangle's sides.

A Script or Meditation Plan. By this we mean that before you count yourself down to the Alpha band, you should already have a very clear idea of how you will organise your visualisation once there. You already know how it ends: the strong image of how things will be. But you won't start with that. Instead you should begin with a simple representation of what you desire, just out of arm's reach. You can then use the ball of light, which grows between you and the representation as it is fed by your desire. It will engulf you both, and you will then see your strong image. It's a simple and effective meditation, but even so, make sure you have the details worked out before you start.

A Schedule. If your desire involves another person or other people, you must tread carefully. Don't repeat too often or too soon. Think of the effects on them, and the consequences those effects could have. Even if the object of your desire is inanimate, there is no need to overdo it. Stick to a schedule of three times a week. Always try and stick to the same time or thereabouts, thus keeping the delays between each process consistent.

A Positive Outlook. For all the reasons we have already examined, you should keep an open mind and a positive outlook both during your meditations, and in the waiting times between as well.

Patience. Sometimes we strike it lucky and the fields are able to manifest our desire very quickly. Most of the time though, there will be a waiting time before you get what you want. Your patience will be required to enable you to keep the required positive outlook.

When planning your process, remember to go for the true desire (which may not be what you immediately think it is) and to then think in terms of that being your goal, rather than any preconceived ideas of how you will reach it.

POTENTIAL USES

Aside from love and money, what else can this incredible process be used for? The answer is almost anything. Here is a selection of ideas based on how some of our clients have successfully used the morphic fields in the past.

Health. Health benefits can range from minor pain relief, or quicker healing of cuts and bruises, right up to helping to treat major diseases, illnesses, or physical problems. Note that we said "helping to treat…" That's because you should *always* consult a doctor or qualified health professional regarding any medical issues. Morphic fields can and do work wonders, and are a great compliment to traditional medicine. But they aren't a replacement, and when dealing with these kinds of issues, frankly why would you not want to use every means of getting well that is available? If you do use the process to help with health issues, focus very much on how you will feel when given the all clear. Don't visualise the problem itself in any way, you'll only give it more energy if you do so. Keep your attention directed towards the things that you will do once the problem has gone away, rather than—say—looking at an infected area and seeing that it has cleared up. This way there is no danger of feeding your problem area with any extra power and attention which could just aggravate the issue.

Friendship. The love process can easily be adapted for good platonic friendship. People are social creatures and contact with others is one of our basic needs. Friends can't always be easy to find or make though. Morphic fields are superb at bringing people together, so why not make a new friend or three?

Family. Most of us have family, and most of us, at some time or another, go through difficult periods with some of those relations. As the old saying goes, you can choose your friends but you can't choose your family. It's expected that we get on well with them, as if our shared DNA should trump any potential difficulties that would strain a regular friendship. But of course we all know in reality that's not true. Family members can sometimes be the most annoying people we know! Yet we are often forced to spend time with them. Christenings, weddings, funerals, and other events mean it is inevitable we run into these people, and we're expected to get along. Even those we are close to and do actually like, can sometimes rub us up the wrong way. A simple morphic field process can smooth these rough times, bringing everyone closer.

Career. Whether you are looking for promotion to reward you for your years of loyal service, or are desperate to change your job after years of being taken advantage of, the fields can help. You have a few ways you can go with this. If you know the position or the job that you want, then be precise about it in your recipe. But if all you know is that you need a change, then you will need to be a bit more cunning. The specific position is easy to do because you can make a nice strong image of yourself in that role. The "get me out of here" scenario means you will have to create a more generic visualisation. It could be, for example, you excitedly telling your partner about how happy you are to have just found your dream job. There is no need to specify the job because we are always interested in looking at the *effect* of achieving the goal much more than we are about seeing the goal itself.

Skill. Want to learn a new language? Or perhaps improve your DIY skills? Maybe you would like to improve your driving to a level whereby you can race? Any skill that can be learnt, can be learnt more quickly with the help of morphic fields. They won't magically implant new knowledge or experience into your brain, Matrix-style, but you will find that you absorb and retain information much more quickly if you use meditation in general, and the morphic field process in particular. Visualise your end goal as having already obtained this knowledge, and how you will feel when you have it.

Lose Weight. Dieting is hard, no matter what all the books try and tell you. The desire for a healthy and shapely body may well be there, but it never seems to be quite strong enough to overcome the temptation for that delicious looking cake, or that large steak, or the chocolate, beer, or whatever else seems to be calling out your name today. Instead of directing that desire at a complicated weight loss plan that requires God-like powers of self control, use it in an Alpha band visualisation. See yourself as having already lost the weight. Picture yourself at your ideal size and shape, and think about what it will mean to you once you've achieved it. When you use morphic fields this way, they aren't going out into the universe, using their infinite connections to locate something you want, instead they will act internally, affecting your very own limbic system bringing about an effect not unlike self hypnosis. You'll find yourself making the right choices about what to eat and when, and it will happen effortlessly. Our clients constantly tell us that weight loss is one of their favourite uses for the morphic field process.

Give Up Smoking. This is another one of those things that requires incredible self control and discipline. As with weight loss, your visualisation will deeply affect you internally, suppressing your cravings. You will quite simply lose the urge to smoke. Of course, the desire to quit must be there, and that is where some struggle. On the surface they say they want to give up, but deep down they enjoy the activity too much. But if you smoke, and you truly want to stop, this process can and will make that happen much more quickly and easily. The same goes for any kind of addiction—alcohol, drugs, sex, gambling—the fields can help with all of them. Of course, we do recommend that if you suffer from any addiction, you should contact a health professional for advice. In any health related matter, morphic fields should be used in addition to, never instead of, regular medicine.

Self Confidence. A lack of confidence in oneself can be debilitating. It can lead to lower job prospects, loneliness, unhappiness, and even poor health in extreme cases. Confidence isn't something we are born with, it's something we learn. But it's a learning process that encompasses all of our life experiences to date. Changing that learnt behaviour pattern normally takes an awful lot of work. The morphic field process is absolutely superb at overcoming this problem. If you suffer from a lack of confidence, start by thinking of a situation that terrifies you, one where the issue is really highlighted. It could be some kind of public speaking, or it could be the idea of asking someone out on a date. Whatever makes you the most afraid, use that. Then turn the situation on its head. Imagine how it would be if you were the most confident person in the world. If you are speaking publicly, imagine the audience being captivated, hanging on your every word, lapping it up. If the thought of asking someone out is what scares you, turn that round and imagine the person not only saying yes, but clearly being genuinely enthused, over the moon that you asked them. The positive image is of course the strong image you will then use in your visualisation. And again, the morphic field energy will work internally to you, building up real confidence within you. Just like the love created by the process in Part One, this confidence is not fake or in any way unreal. It will come about through the exact same chemical reactions in the brain as if you were born with it.

Finding A Soul Mate

In Part Two we studied in detail a process geared around getting a known, named person to fall in love with you. But what if you haven't met that person yet? What if you are searching for a soul mate, the perfect partner, someone you have yet to find?

Happily, morphic fields can help you. After all, you're already connected through them to every other person on the planet.

The recipe you will use for this is more akin to the method for attracting money. We saw in Part Three that by concentrating on the goal rather than a specific source of wealth, we allow the fields free reign to go out into the world and find us a source of money that matches our requirement. You can use the same concept to find a soul mate. By concentrating on the end result, the fields can locate a partner for you.

The first step is to define this partner. With money, you only needed to write down a number, a figure representing the cash you wanted. With a person, it's more involved. You'll need to create a kind of mental model of the person you desire, your soul mate. Some people find this harder than others, but it is a necessary step if you want the fields to do your bidding.

Your mental model does *not* have to include physical attributes; you don't need to visualise an image of what this person looks like (although you can if you want). More important is who this person *is*. Where did they grow up? What did they study? What do they enjoy doing? How do they spend their time? How to they speak? How to they act in different situations? What do they love about you? What drives them crazy? What makes them laugh so hard it hurts? The more specific you can get the better. Maybe you know their job? Where they live? What they like to wear? Their favourite films and books?

It's best to write this all down. A written profile will force you to think about your model in greater detail, and will also act as your mental crutch for the process. You can read through it before each meditation, strengthening your desire.

Your moment of perfection should be easy to visualise. It can be the instant you first meet this person, or it could just be something as simple as a lazy afternoon spent in their company, as long as it fills you with happiness. With all the ingredients prepared, you can continue the process as per the regular love process described in Part Two, with your written mental model replacing the picture.

A word of warning: manifestation for a soul mate can take longer than for a known, named person. The morphic fields have extra work to do here. Before they can connect you to your future partner, they have to find them. The more specific you are in your model, the narrower the field and the longer it may take. It can be tempting then, to keep the field open and just use the process to find "a hot blonde" or "a tall dark hunk", but if you truly desire a soul mate, this is a waste of time. You'll just end up with someone entirely unsuitable, and have to start over. Patience then, as always, is your greatest asset.

One At A Time

Once you have tasted the power that the morphic fields have to offer, and experienced the success of having them manifest your desire, it can be tempting to make a shopping list of all the things you think you want from life, and then spend your days at the Alpha band doing processes for all of them.

This would be a mistake. If you run two processes concurrently, you will be splitting your energy between them. Your manifestation triangle will be weakened, particularly the desire side. Even though you will *want* all the things you are trying to process at once, the desire for any single one will not be strong enough to get the morphic fields working for you. That desire must be concentrated, and that is achieved by focussing on it almost to the exclusion of all other desires. Of course, those other desires never go away while working on one particular thing, but they can be pushed to the back of your mind.

Trying to process more than desire is to try and juggle too many balls at once, you will simply end up dropping them all. It is far more effective to pick one and work on it. Once it manifests, use that to boost your belief system and move on to the next thing on your list. Each success will build on the last, and will see you achieve greater goals more quickly than you ever thought possible.

HELPING OTHERS

So far we have, perhaps selfishly, studied how to use morphic fields for our own gain. But what about helping others? We all have friends and family who we know have problems to deal with. Could we perhaps use our newfound skill to give a brother or sister a financial boost? Or help out an Aunt through a rocky relationship problem?

These things are all possible—to a degree. There are two problems with using the fields for the benefit of others, and they both stem from the desire side of the manifestation triangle. The first issue is that you may think you know the other person's desire, but there is a strong possibility you are mistaken. We have already seen how we lie to ourselves about our *own* true desires. Getting to the bottom of what we really want is hard enough, but finding out what someone else really wants is much harder. You might suspect someone in your family has money worries, they always seem short of cash and have trouble paying their bills. More money could help, but it may just be a short term solution. What if the real problem is that they have a secret addiction to internet poker? Getting more cash into their bank account could actually make the problem worse, as they'll have more to gamble with. Their actual wish would more likely be to overcome their addiction. But as they are keeping it hidden from everyone, you would have no way of knowing that.

Gambling addiction is an extreme example, but it does illustrate how so often we think we know someone and understand their problems, when in reality we have no idea what is really going on. Trying to fix someone else's problems undoubtedly comes from a genuine wish to help and to do the right thing, but it can be misguided.

From a practical point of view, unless the solution to the person's problem as we see it is perfectly aligned with what they truly want, the desire side of the triangle will not be sufficiently strong to bring about manifestation.

The second issue is more straightforward. With the best will in the world, our own desire to see this other person's problem solved is rarely going to be as strong as our desire to fix our own problems, or otherwise enrich our own lives. We are naturally selfish creatures. Evolution has seen to it that our priority is to look after number one. Altruism simply isn't a strong enough motivator to drive the desire side of the triangle.

When we combine these two problems, we see the chance of success diminish drastically. If you really want to help someone else, the single best thing you can do for them is to introduce them to the power of morphic fields. Lend them a copy of this book, or buy one for them as a gift. Or take the time to teach them what you have learned yourself. Tell them, in as much detail as you feel comfortable divulging, about your own successes. It will give their belief system a head start, and as a bonus it will boost your own; recounting your own successes will bring them more into focus for you. Encourage them to share their experiences with you. Having someone close who uses the morphic fields can be a great way to get ideas for new visualisations and uses. Pool your knowledge and experience and you'll both benefit.

Bonus Method:
Insomnia

Recent statistics suggest that more than 30% of the adult population suffer from insomnia to some degree. The knock on effects of a lack of proper sleep seemingly know no bounds. It directly causes dietary problems, lack of energy, poor concentration, poor memory, stress and anxiety, Indirectly it can cause industrial accidents, motoring accidents, and domestic accidents. The stress and strain brought about by tiredness is thought to be responsible for a raft of personal problems including marital issues and even domestic violence.

Anyone who has suffered from insomnia knows that it can become a self fuelling spiral of despair. When you are unable to sleep for nights on end, you begin to fear your bed, knowing that it is not going to bring peace and relaxation. That fear just makes it more difficult to get to sleep.

You can use the morphic field process to help get over insomnia. For your strong image, picture yourself waking up in the morning after the most refreshing night's sleep you've ever had.

But even before the effect of the process kicks in, there is another way you can use the skills you have learnt in this book in order to fall asleep more easily. In fact, if you use the system we are about to share with you every night for a week, you will from then on, be able to go to sleep, at will, anywhere at any time. It sounds too good to be true, but we have both used this system personally for many years, and couldn't imagine life without it. We have individually taught it to countless people, and they too use it daily to fall asleep peacefully and naturally.

The first step is to slow your brainwaves to the Alpha band. When you are in bed (or wherever you decide to sleep), use the countdown meditation to reach Alpha. This alone will take you closer to sleep, your brainwave frequency is already down a notch on the scale, leaving you with less to do to drift off. But we can do much better.

Once at the Alpha band, clear your mind's eye so you see nothing at all. Then in front of you, imagine a dry erase board, the kind used in conference rooms the world over. In the hand you write with is a dry erase marker. In your other hand you have board eraser.

Take the marker and in the middle of the board, write in very large figures the number 100. Don't shortcut this and just imagine the number has appeared, visualise yourself carefully and neatly drawing out each figure. When you have done so, underneath the number, write the word "Sleep". Again, see yourself write out each letter in exacting detail. Finally, starting in the bottom right corner and working clockwise, draw a big rectangle around everything you have written.

Now take the board eraser in your other hand and working from top to bottom, left to right, wipe out everything you just put up on the dry erase board, leaving it blank once again.

Now repeat the process, but write up the number 99. You can probably guess the rest! Each time you erase the board, start again, counting down with every repetition.

The first time—or perhaps the first few times—that you do this, you may get all the way down to 1. If that happens, start again from 100. If you lose your place because your mind wanders, start again from 100.

This is *really* boring, and your brain will object. It will try and think of something, anything else. It will want to day-dream, to think about what you watched on television, or what you are going to do tomorrow. It will even try and think about problems or worries you have right now. It would prefer to dwell on the negative rather than the dull and boring task of writing down these numbers. To stay focussed, you'll need to put all of your concentration into writing those numbers out. If you feel your thoughts drift off elsewhere, bring your attention back to the tip of the marker on the white board. Watch it as it draws out the number. Don't leave any room in your head for other thoughts or ideas to creep in.

Eventually, your subconscious mind will get the message that the only way it is going to escape this dull repetitive task is by going to sleep. It might take a few nights, even a week, for it to get the hint. But once it clicks, the effect is like magic. You'll find that you won't get past 90 in your countdown, before dozing off. And the more you do it, the better it works. We both use this method and rarely see a number lower than 98. The brain sees the 100 and says to itself: "Oh no, not this again, I'm outta here!" and sleep follows immediately.

It's best to start using the method only at night, in bed. Once it has clicked for you though, you can use it any time and any place. Want to sleep for an hour on the train during your commute? Count yourself to Alpha, visualise your whiteboard, and off you go. You can be asleep within two minutes.

ALSO BY THE AUTHOR

Do you want to read tarot, but don't want to wade through piles of long tedious explanations that bore you to tears? *Tarot Made Simple* is a tarot guide for the 21st century. Forget about having to try and memorise page after dull page of metaphysical nonsense, *Tarot Made Simple* explains how the cards really work, and how anyone can start reading them in a day.

If you thought feng shui was complicated, think again! *Five Minute Feng Shui* cuts through the mysticism and the long winded history and gets quickly to the point. This easy-to-follow guide will show you how you can get instant benefits from feng shui.

Made in United States
Troutdale, OR
08/07/2023

11895389R00082